Video Projects for Elementary and Middle Schools

Other Titles by
Keith Kyker and Christopher Curchy

Television Production for Elementary and Middle Schools (1994)

Television Production: A Classroom Approach (1993)
    Instructor Edition
    Student Edition, Book 1: Beginning
    Student Edition, Book 2: Advanced
    Video

Video projects

for Elementary and Middle Schools

Keith Kyker and Christopher Curchy

1995
Libraries Unlimited, Inc.
and its division Teacher Ideas Press
Englewood, Colorado

LIBRARIES UNLIMITED, INC.
and its division
Teacher Ideas Press
P.O. Box 6633
Englewood, CO 80155-6633
(800) 237-6124

Production Editor
Constance Hardesty

Interior Book Design and Composition
Sheryl Tongue

Library of Congress Cataloging-in-Publication Data

Kyker, Keith.
    Video projects for elementary and middle schools / Keith Kyker and
Christopher Curchy.
        xii, 121 p.   22×28 cm.
        Includes index.
        ISBN 1-56308-377-9
        1. Video tapes in education. 2. Television in education.
    3. Elementary schools. 4. Middle schools. I. Curchy, Christopher.
    II. Title.
    LB1044.75.K94   1995
    372.13'358 -- dc20   95–24689
                                                               CIP

Dedications

For all of my new friends in Northwest Florida.
After many years, I am home.
K.K.

For all of my students, elementary through college,
because you helped me realize that you
are the most important component
in any classroom!
C.C.

Acknowledgments

The authors would like to acknowledge
the contributions of the following individuals:
Linda Patterson
Michelle Funnell
Alice Lawson
Kathy Little
Sharon Shirey
Pattie Smith
Jan Weber
Donna Earle
Gloria Bentley

We would especially like to thank
Mike Lalone for his illustrations.

Contents

Chapter 4   Video Projects and Plans *(continued)*

Foreword

Education is both an art and a science. The art of education involves the teacher's heart—caring about students, acting as a facilitator and role model, and advocating for quality instruction. The science of education involves the teacher's head—organizing, scheduling, making administrative decisions, and designing curriculum. Television production involves the heart and the head of the media teacher.

Combining their talents, Christopher Curchy and Keith Kyker offer a cornucopia of helpful suggestions that call on both the heart and the head. They introduce practical ideas that are useful for both novice and experienced media teachers. They have managed to achieve an integration of accessible theory with a thoroughly workable and down-to-earth classroom practice.

Of most help to teachers new to video production are the topics and ideas for student involvement. Developing a video from start to finish, the students use many diverse skills. Reading, writing, researching, learning to work as a team, and public speaking skills complement the vast array of production and critical viewing skills.

Students everywhere should have access to these highly practical ideas, and every media teacher will wish to own a copy. I have great admiration for this project, for it is bound to have an important impact on elementary and middle school classrooms.

Linda S. Patterson
Instructional Communications and Technology
Walton County School District, Florida

Introduction

Elementary students today grow up in a much different world than we did. We were fascinated by the phonograph, the television, the portable AM radio. We had to ask permission to use the telephone.

Today, children use portable FM stereos that sound better than the hi-fi that sat in the family living room 25 years ago. They connect the telephone to the computer and talk with Internet pals around the world. They say, "Mommy, Daddy, what's a record player?"

And they make television.

Boy, do they make television.

The visual nature of television production, coupled with the immediate gratification of watching the just-recorded image through the camcorder viewfinder or on the family TV, makes videography a perfect activity for children and adolescents. Observe any family picnic or Cub Scout gathering, and you will see a child holding a camcorder.

"Foolish to put that expensive camcorder in the hands of a child," you say? We say, 'tis more noble for a parent to buy a camcorder or computer than to buy a souped-up video game system and introduce expensive game cartridges into birthday and holiday celebrations.

Bottom line: Kids learn when using video equipment. They may not be ready to study optical data retrieval or count the pixels on a charge-coupled device. But they learn. They learn about visual literacy. They learn about composition. They learn patience. They learn teamwork. They learn not to drop something expensive ... again.

But most importantly, they learn that television doesn't have to be a spectator sport. Modern technology has made it easy and affordable for children to make the television they want to watch. Nothing on the tube? Make something yourself!

This book is a companion to our recent book, *Television Production for Elementary Schools* (Libraries Unlimited, 1994). *Television Production for Elementary Schools* has been received enthusiastically by elementary and middle school teachers and media specialists. It features chapters about several important topics, including an explanation of the television production process, guidelines for creation of school news shows and orientation tapes, and working with vendors. The book also features 20 student lessons about television production technology and careers. Basically, it is a handbook and curriculum for video production in elementary and middle schools.

This book offers 25 hands-on video projects for students in grades K–8 and tips for creating these projects and integrating them into the curriculum. We strongly recommend using *Television Production for Elementary Schools* as a reference when creating these video projects, just as you would consult a text about architecture before reading house plans. Will this book stand alone? If you have extensive television production experience, you probably can help your students create these projects without depending on the first book. But if you are new to video production or have only a moderate amount of experience, the first book is an invaluable tool.

You may be familiar with our middle/high school text, *Television Production: A Classroom Approach* (Libraries Unlimited, 1993). Schools around the world use the book as a middle, high school, and even college text. The curriculum emphasizes technical and aesthetic aspects of school-based video production, integrating the concepts with hands-on video projects that reinforce the skills learned in each lesson. It gives equal weight to process and product.

It is our belief that television production in elementary and middle schools should be process-oriented, with less emphasis placed on the finished product. Even though your fourth-graders will undoubtedly produce some outstanding video projects, you probably won't get any calls from Hollywood or the major networks. Will Mom and Dad help little Sarah when she uses the family camcorder to create the project *My Pet*? Sure. Is this bad? No. Will it affect her grade? What grade?

In this book, you *will* find 25 video projects. You *won't* find grading sheets. We have provided a section about what to look for in a video project, and reading *Television Production for Elementary Schools* will offer tips on improving your students' video work. But for now, let's resist the temptation to assign a number or letter grade to the students' work. Let's emphasize the process. If you need to grade projects, grade them on creativity and teamwork. Grade students' understanding of the subject matter. And watch students' proud faces as they play their video projects for the class.

Make sure your students know television is not a spectator sport. And make sure they know the importance of that lesson. ■

Chapter 1

Equipment and Techniques for Video Projects

This chapter discusses some basic techniques for creating the video projects described later in this book and briefly explains the use of the equipment required for the projects. This chapter does not serve as a complete explanation of the make-up and use of video production equipment commonly found in elementary and middle schools. For that information, please consult our previous book, *Television Production for Elementary Schools* (Libraries Unlimited, 1994); for a more complete explanation, consult our secondary-level text, *Television Production: A Classroom Approach* (Libraries Unlimited, 1993).

Video Production Equipment

Although video production at the elementary and middle school levels can be done with just a few pieces of equipment, it is important for the teacher or media specialist to understand the features and controls of these items. You probably have most of this equipment at the school already. You may need to purchase peripheral items as their need becomes apparent.

To create good video projects without the frustration that results from not having the tools to do the job, the media specialist should, whenever possible, obtain and use industrial/professional video equipment. Don't let the terms *industrial* and *professional* overwhelm you. There are three grades of television production equipment: broadcast, industrial/professional, and consumer. Obviously, broadcast equipment is used by professional broadcast and cable TV stations. This is the highest level of equipment. The second, or mid-point, level is industrial/professional. Industrial/professional equipment will perform many of the tasks that you would expect from broadcast equipment, including editing, audio dubbing, and frame-by-frame searching. However, the quality is slightly lower than that of broadcast equipment, and the price reflects that difference. The lowest grade is consumer, which includes the camcorders, VCRs, and microphones sold at retail stores. Although the price of this equipment represents value to the consumers who will use their camcorders once or twice a week, it is not a wise investment for an industrial setting, where the equipment will be used extensively every day. As you have probably guessed, the school is an industrial setting.

To further complicate matters, creative marketing and the affordability of industrial equipment has blurred the lines between the three levels. An industrial camcorder that cost $3,000 five years ago can now be purchased for about half that price. And the consumer unit that five years ago cost about $1,500 can now be purchased for about $600. The temptation for schools is to look at price, not quality, saying, "Now I can get this $1,500 camcorder for only $600. What a bargain!" But, of course, there is no bargain, because the school will be purchasing a consumer model that will not withstand the daily wear-and-tear of school-based video production. Instead, the school should be pleased that it can now purchase industrial equipment for the same price as consumer equipment sold for just a few years ago.

This section of chapter 1 examines the following equipment: camcorder, tripod, industrial/professional VCR, microphone, audio mixer, character generator, and television/monitor.

Camcorder

The camcorder is the basic item of equipment in elementary and middle school television production. Most schools already own at least one camcorder, and it is probably used to videotape the morning news show, school plays, and guest speakers. If your school owns only one camcorder, and it is already used extensively, you should consider purchasing a second unit for use in video production. The least expensive industrial/professional camcorder that will perform the tasks described in the following sections can be purchased for about $1,000. After you show your principal all of the great projects you plan to create using this camcorder, he or she will probably agree that the extra unit is a wise investment.

Regular Camcorder Features

Most industrial/professional camcorders have standard features that the teacher and media specialist should learn to use before leading students in these projects. They include: automatic and manual focus, automatic and manual white balance, automatic and manual iris, and servo and manual zoom lens.

Automatic and manual focus. The automatic focus selects a part of the image to be recorded by the camcorder (usually the center of the shot) and brings that part into focus by making slight adjustments in the lens focal length. The manual focus, of course, requires the person using the camcorder to adjust the focus. Select a camcorder that will allow the user to use the manual focus as well as the automatic. Many otherwise acceptable shots are ruined by the automatic focus re-focusing as a tree branch brushes into the shot or the guest speaker takes an unexpected step backward.

Automatic and manual white balance. The white balance of the camcorder controls the way the camera processes and records color. Automatic white balance, or a version of automatic that allows the user to select between indoor and outdoor settings, can be quite valuable in certain situations. For example, if you are videotaping a tree-planting ceremony that begins in the auditorium and progresses to the front of the school, the automatic white balance could be employed to provide continuous white balancing as the videographer walks from the fluorescent light into the natural sunshine. Most other times, though, it is best to use a manual white balance, which is more accurate and produces true colors. (Manual white balancing is usually achieved by pointing the camera at a white object—the wall or a note card, for example—and pushing the white balance button.) Select a camera that offers manual white balance, and teach students how to use this simple function.

Automatic and manual iris. Most camcorders have reasonably large lenses that gather large amounts of light. However, the lens is rarely wide open on the inside. The lens opening, called the aperture, is controlled by a mechanism called the lens iris. Most camcorders are equipped with an automatic iris. In other words, the iris automatically evaluates the available light and adjusts the size of the aperture accordingly. Under low-light conditions, the aperture is quite large—about the size of a half-dollar. In the bright sunshine, the aperture may be as small as the tip of a pencil. In many cases, this automatic iris produces an excellent video picture. In some instances, though, the automatic iris betrays the videographer. The most easily understood example involves videotaping a guest speaker who is standing in a spotlight in front of a dark background. The automatic iris does its best to provide a clear, bright picture of the entire shot. By opening the aperture to brighten the unlit background, the automatic iris allows too much light into the camcorder, making the guest speaker's face overly bright and totally washed out. You can probably think of several other situations in which this could happen. Select a camcorder with a manual override for the automatic iris, and use it when necessary.

Servo and manual zoom lens. The servo zoom lens featured on almost all camcorders manufactured today is a motorized lens that allows smooth, effortless zooming in and out by pressing the *T* (telephoto) or *W* (wide-angle) buttons positioned near the trigger. To achieve a quicker zoom, presumably when the videographer is not rolling tape, the manual zoom can be employed. Using the manual zoom can increase the creativity required by advanced video projects and on-the-go videography.

Editing Features

Most industrial/professional camcorders are capable of interfacing with an industrial/professional VCR and an editing control unit to form an editing system. Many schools are able to save money by using a camcorder as a play or record deck in the editing process. The editing features available on camcorders include audio insert (audio dub), assemble, and video insert (video dub).

Audio insert (audio dub). Audio insert refers to the process of erasing the audio tracks on the videotape and replacing them with new audio. The process, often referred to as audio dub, can be performed using many camcorders. Later, this chapter explains the process of audio dubbing (pages 17–20). Many teachers and school media specialists currently own camcorders capable of audio dubbing but have never used that feature.

Assemble. An assemble edit records new audio, video, and control track onto the videotape. When copying a program onto a videotape, you are essentially performing a long assemble edit. Many teachers and media specialists connect two VCRs in a deck-to-deck editing configuration. This process is inexpensive and not tremendously accurate. Adding an editing control unit allows users to pinpoint the positions of assemble edits to within a fraction of a second of the desired edit location on the videotape.

Video insert (video dub). Many camcorders will perform a video insert, or video dub. The video insert replaces one section of video with another without erasing the audio tracks or the control track. The technique can be especially useful when trying to spice up a long interview or comment in the editing process.

For a complete discussion of editing in the elementary/middle school setting, consult *Television Production for Elementary Schools*.

Inputs and Outputs

Important to the editing process is the availability on the camcorder of inputs and outputs for audio and video signals. Consumer camcorders often skimp on this feature, but most industrial/professional camcorders have audio and video inputs and outputs.

Using shielded patch cable, the camcorder can be connected to a VCR to complete an editing configuration. Separate inputs indicate that the camcorder can be used as a recording VCR or a play VCR in the editing process. Consult our previous texts for a full description of editing connections and techniques.

Review

To review this section: whenever possible, select an industrial/professional camcorder; be aware of the manual and automatic features of your camcorder; use the camcorder for editing by connecting the inputs or outputs to a VCR.

Tripod

The tripod is one of the least expensive ($75–150), easiest-to-operate, and most valuable parts of your school video program.

So, you think you don't need a tripod? How long can an elementary or middle school student stand still? I rest my case. Humor aside, no one, regardless of age, can be expected to hold a steady camera shot for more than a minute or two. Whenever you or your students are videotaping a shot that lasts more than a few seconds, use a tripod. This includes longer video projects, macro projects, and news shows. Tripods generally are not required for short (one-minute) interviews or informal shots taken in the school.

When using a tripod, make sure its height is right. Adjust the tripod's height so the camera lens is level with your subject's eyes. Many camera operators fail to adjust the height of the tripod to follow the common sense rules that apply to all videography. For example, in many elementary news shows, the news reader sits at a table, with eye level at about 3 feet, but the camera is on a tripod about 5 feet tall. This uncomfortable downward angle shows the top of the news reader's head and little else. Lower the tripod (either the legs or the center pole, called the pedestal) so the camera lens is at your subject's eye level.

A tripod dolly is a good companion to the tripod. Most dollies are three casters or small wheels connected by a metal base. The dolly attaches to the feet of the tripod, allowing the tripod and camera to be rolled during the shot or between shots for easier repositioning. Tripod dollies cost about as much as a tripod.

Here are some tips for buying a tripod: Make sure the tripod will support the weight of your camera. Most tripods have a maximum weight limit (see the tripod's manual for this information), and the camcorder manual will tell you the camcorder's weight. Select a tripod that breaks down to a manageable size for easy transportation. Make sure your tripod has a quick-release mechanism, which allows easy attachment of the camera to the tripod. Finally, select a tripod that doesn't have too many loose parts (screws or wing nuts, for example) that can and will be lost.

If you don't own a tripod for your school camcorder, put down this book immediately, complete the purchase order, and buy that tripod. Got one? Good. Read on.

Industrial/Professional Videocassette Recorder

An industrial/professional VCR is a valuable addition to any school video production program. Such a VCR represents a sizable investment (about $1,000). Some key features of the typical industrial/professional VCR are four-head recording, video and audio inputs and outputs, a jog-shuttle wheel, and various editing features.

Four-head Recording

Industrial/professional VCRs use four heads in the recording process. The fourth head, commonly called a flying-erase head, is engaged when the VCR is put on pause or still-frame. This flying erase head gives a clear still-frame and is essential for making pinpoint edits.

Video and Audio Inputs and Outputs

Industrial/professional VCRs offer more than one set of inputs and outputs. Having multiple audio and video inputs allows for connection of two or more separate sources (Source A, Source B, and so forth) that can be selected with a flip of a switch. Video outputs can be connected to video monitors, video projectors, and other VCRs. Audio outputs can be connected to other VCRs for editing or to monitors or amplifiers.

Jog-shuttle Wheel

Most industrial/professional VCRs are equipped with a jog-shuttle wheel, which allows for searching and cueing videotape. On many VCRs the jog-shuttle wheel is activated by pressing a button. Wheel operation is generally clockwise for forward and counterclockwise for reverse.

Editing Features

Most industrial/professional VCRs are capable of performing audio and video edits, as well as interfacing with an editing control unit. This editing capability may allow schools to connect the VCR to a camcorder for precise edits. The purchase of another industrial/professional VCR and an editing control unit creates an editing system.

Microphones

One of the most frequently overlooked elements of video production is audio. The next time you watch television, notice how much attention is given to audio. Music, dialog, sound effects, and laugh tracks—all are meticulously recorded on the average situation comedy. News, sports, and drama shows also pay careful attention to audio.

Selecting the Right Microphone

In the school setting, the microphone is the most basic, the most used, and the most misunderstood item of video equipment. Let's take a moment to consider the microphone in terms of the video projects that you are about to create.

First, all microphones are not created equal, nor are they meant to be. Obviously, price and quality come into play. In addition, various microphones are manufactured for very different uses in video production.

Microphones can be categorized two ways: by their element and by their directionality. The element is the part of the microphone that actually converts the sound to an audio signal. There are two types of elements widely used in schools today: the dynamic element and the condenser element. (Other types of elements are used in professional applications.) The condenser microphone produces the best sound quality and is the more expensive of the two. But the condenser microphone can be damaged by rough handling and usually distorts loud noises like yelling students and marching bands. The dynamic microphone is not very expensive and is sturdier than a condenser microphone. The sound quality is not as good, but the dynamic has no trouble processing loud sounds. Examine your needs and your funding, and choose a microphone—dynamic or condenser—accordingly.

The second characteristic that defines categories of microphone is directionality. Usually, microphones are either omnidirectional or unidirectional. Omnidirectional microphones pick up sounds equally well from a 360-degree radius around the microphone. Unidirectional microphones pick up sounds mostly from the front of the microphone, not much from the sides or the back. The unidirectional pattern is sometimes called the cardioid pattern because its sound pick-up pattern is heart-shaped. Some more expensive microphones offer an extra switch that changes the microphone from omnidirectional to unidirectional. You can probably imagine situations when the omnidirectional and unidirectional microphones should be used.

Combining the two categories yields four types of microphones:

- dynamic omnidirectional
- dynamic unidirectional
- condenser omnidirectional
- condenser unidirectional

For morning news shows, a unidirectional microphone on your camcorder would be ideal. But most camcorder-mounted microphones are omnidirectional. In almost all cases, it is necessary to attach an external microphone to the camcorder to record good-quality source-based sound.

Connecting the Microphone

After selecting the best microphone for the intended application, connect the microphone to the camcorder. This sounds simple enough, and in most cases it is. Most camcorders have a microphone jack near the camcorder's permanent microphone. The microphone jack is probably ⅛-inch mini (the size used on headphones for personal stereos). If your microphone's plug is not that size, use an adapter. Adapters can be purchased at most retail electronics stores.

Most microphone plugs measure ⅛ inch or ¼ inch. So, most adapting will be from a microphone with a ¼-inch phone plug into the camcorder's ⅛-inch mini jack. That adapter is readily available. However, the weight of the microphone cable plus the weight of the adapter will probably damage the small microphone camcorder jack. There are two ways to avoid breaking the delicate microphone connector inside the camcorder: (1) wrap the microphone cable around the camcorder handle to relieve the weight on the microphone jack; (2) when purchasing the adapter, also purchase a 6-foot length of mini-connector microphone extension cable. Connect the adapter between the microphone and the extension cable. This way, the plug connecting to the camcorder is not a big ¼-inch plug plus a heavy adapter, but a single mini plug.

Tips for Microphone Use

Here are some tips that will make microphones work better and last longer:

- Teach students to treat microphones carefully.
- Be careful with the microphone cord. Don't coil the cord for storage.
- Mic a source, not an area. The correct microphone-to-source distance is 6 inches.
- Do not allow students to blow, spit on, or tap the surface of a microphone. This causes more damage than 100 drops.

Remember, most microphones cost more to repair than replace. Treat microphones with care, and they will last for many years.

Audio Mixers

In many instances, you will wish to combine the sound of two or more microphones with other music sources to increase the informational and emotional effectiveness of a video project. An audio mixer can select and combine different sound sources to add a professional touch to your programs.

Audio Mixer Inputs

An audio mixer has several jacks that allow the input of audio from various sources. The two types of audio inputs are microphone inputs and line inputs. A good audio mixer should have at least three microphone inputs and at least three line inputs.

Microphone inputs. As the name indicates, microphone inputs accommodate the microphones used in video production. Three is the minimum number of microphone inputs for a good audio mixer. Imagine a video project that would require two narrators—there go the first two microphone inputs. Imagine that a third student wants to play the flute to accompany the narration. There goes the third microphone jack. It is not difficult to imagine projects that would call for even more microphone jacks! "At least three" is a good rule to follow when selecting an audio mixer.

The size of the microphone jacks is also an issue, albeit a minor one, with so many adapters readily available. The most common size for microphone jacks on industrial audio mixers is the ¼-inch phone jack.

More important than the size of the microphone jack is the impedance level for which it is designed. Audio equipment (including microphones and audio mixers) is rated as either high impedance (HiZ) or low impedance (LoZ). The impedance refers to the strength of the signal flow, which is too complicated and not important enough to explain here. The major issue with impedance is that high impedance and low impedance equipment is not compatible. HiZ microphones will not work with a LoZ mixer, and LoZ microphones will not work with a HiZ mixer. A few audio mixers and fewer microphones have switchable impedance, meaning that the user can flip a switch to change from one impedance rating to the other.

Most LoZ microphones use an XLR connector instead of the ¼-inch phone jack used in most HiZ audio applications—but that is not a rule. You must determine the impedance rating of each microphone and your audio mixer. Generally speaking, LoZ is used in broadcast and performance applications (for example, TV studio or concert hall), and HiZ is used in schools and homes. (Usually, HiZ equipment is less expensive.) Impedance can be converted using a special impedance adapter, but this adds cost to your system. Know the equipment's impedance before you purchase new equipment.

Each microphone connection has a corresponding fader (slide control) or potentiometer (a volume knob) on the front of the audio mixer. By carefully adjusting these controls, you can mix the microphones in the desired combination.

Line inputs. A good audio mixer includes at least three line inputs. A line input accommodates sources for prerecorded music and sound effects. Sources for line inputs include

- audiocassette players
- compact disc (CD) players
- VCRs (use the audio out of the VCR)
- laser disc players (use the audio out of the laser disc player)
- multimedia computers (use the line-out or speaker jack on the computer).

Each line source can be connected to a line input of the audio mixer. The standard line input jacks on audio mixers are stereo phono connectors (RCA patch cords). You may need to purchase adapters when using line inputs because of the various jacks and plugs used in audio equipment. As with the microphone inputs, a corresponding fader or potentiometer appears on the audio mixer control panel. By combining microphone and line inputs, you can create some surprisingly professional programs with your audio mixer.

NOTE: Be aware of your school district's policy governing the use of prerecorded audio in video programs. Most prerecorded music is protected by copyright.

Audio Mixer Outputs

The object of the audio-mixing game is to combine all of the inputs into one audio signal. So, even if you have more than 50 microphone and line inputs on your audio mixer (reality check—this *is* a school), don't expect to see a large number of audio outputs; you need only one! The main audio output of the audio mixer (sometimes labeled "main out" or "line out") should be connected to the input of the recording device (the VCR or camcorder). Some audio mixers have another output to accommodate a second recording device or a loudspeaker, but most have only one output.

Audio Mixer Features

A good audio mixer has a few features that help the user complete a good sound mix. They include cue function, cross-fader, balance, and VU meters.

Cue function. The cue function allows the user to hear an audio source through the headphones without selecting the audio source for mixing. Usually, the cue function is controlled by the cue button, located near the fader or potentiometer of each line input. (The cue button is sometimes labeled "solo" or "audio preview.") Pressing this button sends the audio (music, for example) for that line input through the headphones. This feature is especially useful when two music selections from the same audio cassette program are used in a continuous video production. After the conclusion of the first song, the user can pull down the fader, depress the cue button, and search the audiocassette for the next song. When the song is found, the cue button can be reset to allow selection of that line input.

Cross-fader. A cross-fader is a fader control that allows a smooth transition from one line input to another. In other words, using a cross-fader, the audio technician can fade-in the CD player while fading-out the audiocassette player. On the audio mixer, the cross-fader is found between two line input fader controls.

Balance. Many audio mixers are stereo; they send a separate signal to the right and left channels. Many stereo audio mixers allow the user to select where to send the audio signal—to the left channel, the right channel, or both. This selection is made by using the balance control, which usually is a dial above each microphone and line input.

VU meters. A VU (volume unit) meter allows the audio technician to adjust the microphone and line input to the optimum levels. The VU meters may be either analog (like a car speedometer) or LED (little lights). In either case, the boundary between the normal area of the VU meter and the "red" area is 100 percent. The VU meter should approach the red area but not go into it. A VU meter that strays into the red continuously represents a distorted signal. A VU meter that never approaches the red represents a low-level, hollow-quality signal.

Character Generators

Over the past few years, character generators have become less expensive and more powerful, with more features and capabilities. As a result, many elementary and middle schools are purchasing them. A character generator allows the user to type titles and graphics on the screen. Manufacturers may call character generators video titlers, video typewriters, graphics generators, or other similar names. Don't be confused by the name game. Examine the character generator and assess the machine's features before purchasing.

Do not be dismayed if you don't have a character generator and haven't made plans to purchase one. *Television Production for Elementary Schools* offers some useful tips to create graphics without a character generator.

Character Generator Backgrounds

Most character generators offer two background choices: solid color and transparent. With the solid color background, letters and other graphics are typed on a solid-color background. (The background may be blue, red, or any other color.) Some character generators also offer gradient-color backgrounds and texture or patterns.

The transparent background feature allows the user to select "transparent" as a background color. When a camcorder or VCR is connected to the input of the character generator and the transparent background is selected, the signal sent from the camcorder or VCR becomes the background for the graphic. This allows one to use the character generator to type labels like the ones seen on professional news programs. This is critical to making good videos. Buy only character generators that offer the transparent option.

Character Generator Connections

The character generator can function as part of a video production system as well as a stand-alone graphics system. Here is a simple explanation of character generator connections.

In general terms, a character generator has one input and two outputs. The input of the character generator can be any video source; a camcorder signal and a VCR signal are the two most common. The first character generator output is the main output, or line out. This is the output that goes to another VCR for recording. The other character generator output is preview out. A video monitor is connected to the preview out so the user can see graphics before they are selected to go to the line out.

Example: The elementary school news show. A student is seated at a table facing the single camcorder. A cable runs from the video output of the camcorder to the input of the character generator. A transparent background is selected. The character generator operator watches the preview monitor to ensure that the correct graphic has been selected and is ready for use. At the appropriate time (perhaps a few seconds into the show), the character generator operator taps a key to activate the graphic. As the camcorder's signal is processed by the character generator, the graphic is added. The signal is recorded on a VCR via a cable connected to the main output of the character generator and the video input on the VCR. (In this set-up, the audio is recorded by connecting a microphone to an audio mixer, then sending the audio mixer output to the audio input of the recording VCR; see figure 1.1.)

At this point, it is important to note that the video signal is not the radio frequency (RF) signal processed by television sets. An RF signal is modulated and contains both audio and video signals. A cable TV signal, like a broadcast

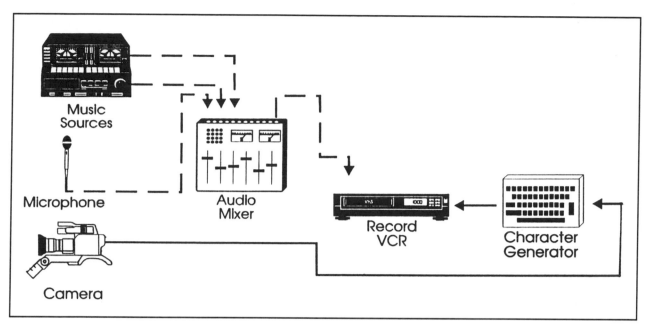

Figure 1.1 A character generator is connected to other audio and video equipment.

TV signal, is an RF signal. Video signal is not modulated and contains only the video, not the audio. Video signal cannot be processed by a television set. For that, a monitor is required.

Televisions and Monitors

After students make their great video projects, we need to watch them. And, students probably want to watch their programs while they are being recorded as well. To do this, you need a television or a monitor. To confuse matters, they are not the same. A television processes an RF signal. The RF signal is a composite signal, which means it contains both audio and video signal. The RF signal is produced by television stations and cable television companies. Many different RF signals can enter your television through a single antenna or cable TV wire that attaches to the back of the television. The tuner on your television set allows you to select which RF signal, or channel, to watch.

A video monitor, on the other hand, processes video signal. Video signal contains only the image. Video signal is created by camcorders, VCRs, and character generators. Because only one video signal enters a video monitor, it does not require a tuner. And, because the video monitor processes only the image, it may not have an audio speaker, either.

In years past, a monitor was a monitor and a television was a television; no exceptions. Fortunately, combination television/monitors are now readily available. The television/monitor has two inputs on the back: RF-in for RF signal and video-in for video signal. Most television/monitors also offer audio-in jacks for input from an audio mixer or the audio-out jack on a VCR. Access to the video and audio signal is usually accomplished by pressing a button on the television/monitor or tuning the television/monitor one notch below channel 2, to a channel labeled A/V (for audio/video). Television/monitors are only slightly more expensive than regular televisions, and they are well worth the investment. With increasing use of the camcorder in the classroom, instructors need equipment that can process the video signal.

Making Macro Projects

A macro project is a video project in which still pictures, drawings, photographs, or realia are recorded in a certain sequence using a camcorder (with the lens in the macro setting) mounted on a tripod.

Here's an example based on the old reliable first-week-of-school project, "How I Spent My Summer Vacation." The students bring in regular snapshot-size photographs of their summer, tape or tack each photograph to the wall, and then videotape each photograph, pausing the camcorder between shots. (The process will be explained in detail in the sections that follow.) Some macro projects include titles and credits (created electronically or by hand), background music, and a narrated script.

Why Make Macro Projects?

There are many advantages to making macro projects.

1. They are very simple to do. They don't require extensive camera skills or post-production experience. Students of any age can make macro projects.

2. Macro projects can revitalize old, trite school assignments, such as "A Famous Scientist" or "My Favorite Book."

3. Macro projects teach writing and composition skills as well as visual literacy, speaking, and music appreciation.

4. Macro projects can be made with a minimum of video equipment. All that is really needed is a camcorder that can audio dub, a tripod, and a monitor.

5. Macro projects are fun. They give students a chance to introduce themselves and their interests to the class, and they provide a valuable educational experience.

6. Macro projects teach rudimentary video production skills in a controlled environment. Students creating macro projects learn about the macro lens, focus, manual iris, tripod, composition, scriptwriting and performance, and audio mixing.

7. Macro projects boost students' confidence, because there is very little chance of failure.

Macro projects are great for faculty projects, too. How many of us have seen our classes disrupted beyond recovery as we try to share snapshots and postcards with our students? Passing around items rarely works; often, the lesson concludes before the unfortunate student in the back of the room sees the first visual. Faculty members can make a macro project using their photos and postcards and share the video on a classroom television/monitor. Using the pause button on the VCR gives the instructor time to talk about each photograph. Music that reflects the content can be added to increase viewers' enjoyment as the tape is watched a second time for review. (Several teachers of geography and foreign language use this technique exclusively for sharing personal visuals with students.) Television is an increasingly effective media with today's students.

Equipment for Making Macro Projects

The Macro Lens

To make a macro project, you need a camcorder with a macro lens. On most camcorders, the macro lens is an additional lens installed within the zoom lens. The macro lens allows up-close videography of very small objects. Using a macro lens, a penny or a postage stamp can be videotaped to fill the monitor screen.

Have you ever tried to videotape a close-up of a small object without using the macro lens? It is impossible. Any objects closer than 2–3 feet will not come into focus, regardless of the zoom setting or focus. That's why most camcorders feature a macro lens.

To use the macro lens, consult your camcorder's manual. Most macro lens adjustments are made on the manual zoom part of the lens. Generally, the user must zoom out all the way, then push a button on the lens casing. Access to this feature varies greatly among manufacturers. Some digital cameras offer a different version of the macro lens. On these cameras, the user zooms out to the widest angle and presses the auto-focus function. The camera then digitally focuses in the macro setting. Whichever focusing system your camera uses, the macro feature will be explained in its instruction manual.

Other Equipment

In addition to a camcorder or a camera-deck system with a macro lens or digital macro capability, equipment needed to produce macro projects includes:

- an adapter to access a video out signal, if needed.
- a tripod.
- a video monitor. If you don't have a monitor, you can use a television with an RF modulator. An RF modulator, which turns the video signal from a camcorder into the RF signal that the TV needs, can be purchased at most electronics stores for less than $20.
- a length of shielded cable to connect the camcorder's video output to the monitor's video input. If you're using a TV with an RF modulator, use this cable to connect the camcorder to the RF modulator. Use another cable to connect the RF modulator to the TV. Check the equipment to determine the connecting ends that need to be on each length of cable; be sure to buy cables that have the right connectors, or buy adapters if you need them. Cables and adapters should be available at any electronics store.

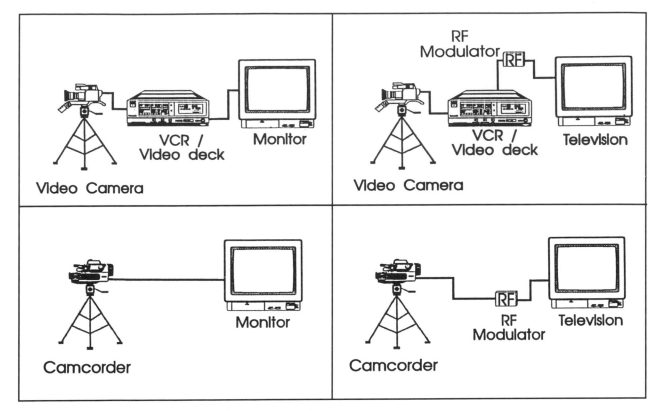

Figure 1.2   Connection options for making macro projects.

Connecting the Equipment

Figure 1.2 shows four options for equipment set-ups for making macro projects. Regardless of what option you use, the following steps apply:

1. Mount the camcorder on the tripod. Adjust the tripod so the camera is level (not tilting up or down).

2. Adjust the tripod height to the chest level of the user. Adjust the center pedestal, not the tripod legs.

3. Position the camera so that the lens is about 6 inches from the wall or bulletin board onto which you will mount the objects for videotaping.

4. Locate the video-out jack on your camcorder. Attach a shielded cable to that output. Attach the other end of that shielded cable to the video-in of your video monitor.

    If you are using a television instead of a monitor, connect the shielded cable to the video-in of the RF modulator. Then run another shielded cable from the RF modulator's output to the antenna input on the television. Tune the television to the channel designated by the RF modulator—probably channel 3 or 4.

5. Turn on the camcorder, television/monitor, and RF modulator (if needed).

6. Remove the lens cap on the camcorder. At this point, you should see a picture from the camcorder on the monitor or TV.

NOTE: Some older camcorders require tape insertion before they will produce a picture. If you don't get a picture on the television/monitor, troubleshoot step 4. (Hints: Check all connections. Make sure you are using video, not audio, ins and outs. Make sure the camcorder is on. Make sure the TV is tuned to the correct channel.)

Making a Macro Project

After connecting the equipment, produce the macro project using the following steps:

1. Using a small amount of masking tape, affix the photo, postcard, or realia to a wall, bulletin board, or other mounting surface. (For simplicity's sake, these instructions use photographs mounted on a wall as an example.)

2. Insert a blank videotape in the camcorder. With the lens cap on, begin recording. Record at least 30 seconds to make a black leader. Pause the camcorder.

    Throughout the project's production, you will be recording audio, even if you don't plan to use it as live sound. To avoid recording sound, you can create the project in a quiet place or insert an adapter—but no microphone—into the microphone jack on the camcorder. This will disable the camcorder's internal microphone.

3. Remove the lens cap and look at the monitor. To fill the frame, move the camcorder forward or backward to accommodate the size of the photo. Don't worry about the focus at this point. Then move the photo up, down, or sideways on the mounting surface so the desired area is centered in the monitor. It is easier to move the photo than the camcorder (see figure 1.3).

4. Now focus. Check the distance between the object and the camera lens. Is it less than 3 feet? If so, you probably need to select the macro lens. Press the appropriate buttons to engage the macro lens. Then focus until the picture becomes sharp and clear. Consult the equipment manual for focusing instructions, which may be different for the macro lens than for the regular or zoom lenses.

5. Press the camcorder trigger, un-pausing the camcorder. Record the photo for the desired time (at least 10 seconds, or as long as you need for narration). Press the trigger again to pause the camcorder.

6. Continue with each photo until your project is complete.

7. Replace the lens cap to record at least 30 seconds of black at the end of your project.

Tips for Creating Macro Projects

Title cards. You may want to use a title to begin your project. Title cards can be made using markers and note cards. Trim an inch off the width of a 3-×-5-inch note card, making it a 3-×-4-inch note card; this will fit the screen

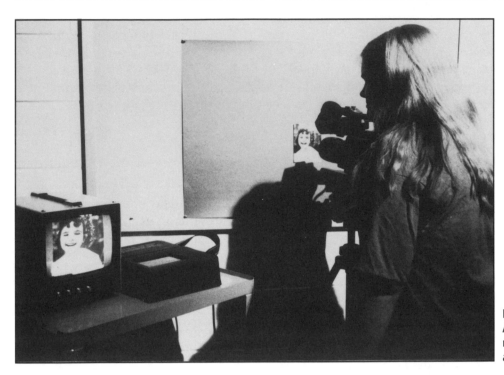

Figure 1.3
An external monitor
makes positioning
and focusing easier.

better. Decorate the card with markers, stickers, and glitter. Then videotape the card as you would any picture.

Fade in and fade out. Fading in and out can enhance macro projects. Fade in on the first shot (picture or title card) and fade out on the last picture. Avoid fading in and out of every shot, or your project will look like a dream sequence from a bad soap opera. Your camcorder may be equipped with a fade button. If not, you can use the manual iris control to achieve fades. Consult the equipment manual for use of these features.

Fill the screen. When positioning the camcorder, try to fill the screen with the picture. Decide what you want your audience to see in the picture, and make that the dominant part of the screen image.

Cropping. You can cut out parts of the photograph that aren't really important and select the parts that are. The camera can be physically moved forward or backward to feature one or two people in a group photograph. Refocusing will be necessary. Moving the camera from the center to one side is another way to zero in on certain parts of the photograph or object. Also, a small matte (available from photography or art-supply stores) can block out unwanted sections of a photograph while framing the desired part.

Background. Sometimes, the camcorder positioning warrants overhang, that is, videotaping so that the photograph does not fill the screen. To make overhang shots look their best, tape your photographs onto a piece of background material taped to the mounting surface. Felt squares work well in this application; they are inexpensive and can be purchased from craft and fabric stores. When the overhang is necessary, the audience will see the background felt, not the school wall.

Making it stick. Use poor-quality—that's right, poor-quality—masking tape to affix your pictures to the background. Poor-quality masking tape has very little glue and doesn't leave a sticky residue when removed. Because the picture will be on the felt for just a few seconds, one small piece of tape should do the trick. Too much tape can ruin heirloom photographs. Also, make sure to remove all masking tape before storing your pictures.

Students helping students. Macro projects are great activities for cooperative learning. Group members can take turns with the tasks of focusing, applying the masking tape, and positioning the camera. However, be sure that one or two students are not allowed to dominate other children's projects. Unfortunately, some students can be quite critical, with comments like "You're using *that* picture?" Make sure each student has the opportunity to create his or her own project. Students can help other students by applying and removing masking tape and keeping the pictures in order. As the instructor, make sure that "helpers" don't become "directors."

Audio Dubbing

Audio dubbing is the process of recording a new audio track (sound) onto an existing video program. Audio dubbing can be very useful when you wish to add narration or music to video projects. Audio generally increases the value of video projects and allows them to stand alone without introduction or explanation by the instructor.

Audio dubbing is not the same as recording on a VCR or camcorder. Determine if your video equipment has audio dub functions. If it does not, you will not be able to audio dub. Pressing the record button while speaking into the microphone has disastrous results, erasing both the video and the audio sections of your project. Audio dub is a specific function and cannot be substituted by the record function.

Audio Dub Connections

As long as you have a camcorder with audio dubbing capability, the equipment is minimal and the process is fairly easy. In this section, using a camcorder to audio dub will be explained first, followed by audio dubbing using an industrial/professional VCR. These discussions assume voice-only audio dub. Mixing voice and another sound, such as music, requires use of an audio mixer during the audio dub. Discussion of the equipment needed for that process concludes this section.

Audio Dubbing Using a Camcorder

Most camcorders, beyond the most rudimentary, feature an audio dub function. To connect the equipment:

1. Connect the microphone to the camcorder's microphone input.

2. Connect your monitor or television to the video output of the camcorder. (See the discussion of equipment for producing macro projects on page 13.)

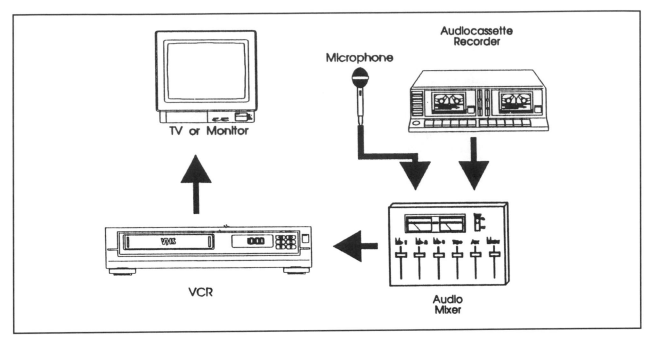

Figure 1.4   Audio dub connections for voice and music, using an audio mixer.

   3. Locate the camcorder's audio-out jack. Run a cable from this jack to the audio-in jack on the monitor. If you are using a television/RF modulator, the audio runs through the RF modulator, too. (See step 4 on page 14.)

Audio Dubbing Connections Using an Industrial/Professional VCR

   1. Locate the microphone jack on the VCR. Connect the microphone.

   2. Connect a monitor or television to the VCR. Run a cable from the video-out of the VCR to the video-in of the monitor. Do the same with the audio connections. If you are using a TV instead of a monitor, you probably won't need the RF modulator required by camcorder users. Most VCRs have built-in RF modulators. Instead of using the audio/video connects, just run a cable from the RF-out jack on the VCR to the antenna input of your television, and tune the television to the appropriate channel—usually 3 or 4.

Audio Dubbing Connections Using an Audio Mixer

Using music and voice or adding additional narrators requires the use of an audio mixer. Here's how to connect the audio mixer for the audio dub process (see figure 1.4):

   1. Connect either the camcorder or the industrial/professional VCR to the television/monitor.

   2. Connect all audio sources (microphones or music sources) to the audio mixer inputs. (See pages 7–8.)

3. Connect the output of the audio mixer (line out or main out) to the VCR or camcorder.

If you are using an industrial/professional VCR, use the audio inputs.

For a camcorder, if it has audio inputs, use them. Otherwise, use the microphone jack. Using the microphone jack will probably require the use of the mic/line adapter included in the accessory packet of the camcorder. Consult the equipment manual for the specifics.

The Audio Dub Process

Don't make a valued project your first audio dub. Instead, shoot some footage around school and practice audio dubbing over that footage. Also, read the camcorder or VCR manual's instruction about audio dubbing before you begin the process. Most camcorders and VCRs audio dub in the way described below, but there are exceptions to every rule! Finally, remember that all existing audio is lost during the audio dub process. Any natural sound will be erased.

Follow these steps for a painless audio dub.

1. Insert a videotape into the VCR or camcorder. Begin to play the tape. You should see the image on your monitor or VCR.

2. Find the place on the videotape where you want to begin the audio dub. Pause the VCR or camcorder.

3. While the VCR or camcorder is on play-pause, press the audio dub button. The VCR or camcorder is now on audio dub-pause.

4. Press the pause button to un-pause the VCR or camcorder. You are now audio-dubbing. Begin the music or narration.

5. If using an audio mixer, fade-out the music as the last shot fades.

REMEMBER: Do not press the record button during the audio dub process, or you will erase the video as well as the existing audio.

Audio Dubbing Tips

Begin before. Begin your audio dub a few seconds before your program actually appears on the screen. This will erase any ambient sound recorded during your 30 seconds of black. Beginning the audio dub before the first image appears allows your audience to view a few seconds of silent black before your program begins. Do the same at the end of your program, audio dubbing silence after the conclusion of the video.

Narrating the script. Practice, practice, practice! Encourage students to practice their scripts aloud several times before the audio dubbing process. Students should practice aloud, not silently or in a whisper. They should practice narrating while they watch the tape, so they can adjust their timing to match the images (see figure 1.5).

Make sure that the narrator is comfortable with the pronunciation of all words, especially if encyclopedia research was involved. Help students find simpler words that substitute for the difficult ones.

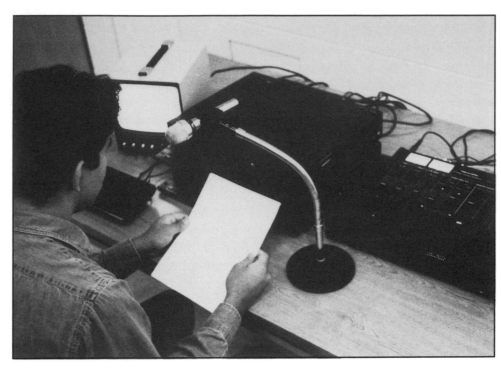

Figure 1.5
Students should practice
narrating while watching
the tape.

Try to arrange a quiet, private place for student audio dubs. Many students will become nervous and flustered if they have to perform an audio dub with the entire class listening and watching.

Warn students against rustling script papers. Students can copy scripts on note cards to avoid rustling paper noises.

Provide a microphone stand so that microphone handling noises will not be heard during the audio dub.

Audio mixing. If music is used with the narration, allow students to practice mixing the voice and music. Use a practice videotape to let students attempt the audio dub. Allow students to play and critique their practice sessions. Provide headphones for the audio mixer; the television/monitor audio will be distracting to the narrator and will probably produce squealing feedback.

Selecting music. Guide your students to music that will add to their projects. Some music is just not appropriate in the school setting; other tunes are safe but don't fit the project. Consider purchasing copyright-cleared music for use in student projects. Learn about your district's copyright policy as it applies to the use of music in nonstudent-produced video projects.

Audio dubbing is a skill that is perfected with experience. Teach audio dubbing as a skill to the entire class and be prepared to review with each group. Plan to practice audio dubbing using practice videotapes before audio dubbing your valuable project, and allow students to do the same.

Evaluation of Video Projects

This book is not about grades. It is about getting the tools of television production in the hands of students and teaching them video is a medium of expression, not a spectator sport. However, if you decide to spend several classroom hours working on a project, you probably will want to give students a grade for their efforts.

Elementary and middle school students are quite capable of creating television programs—generating ideas, imagining shots and special effects, and selecting music. Unfortunately, the students' video production abilities and the school's equipment usually falls short of the standards that spawned those dreams. Undertake the process of grading very carefully, taking into account students' fragile egos and looking beyond the shaky camera work and unsophisticated narration. See the hard work, diligence, and creativity in every frame.

Video production is useful in two school situations: the elementary or middle school media production class and the content-area class in which the instructor has decided to allow students to work with video. Media production instructors probably are more interested in production technique than are content instructors, who focus on content.

Philosophies of Grading Video Projects

Philosophies or approaches to grading video projects are determined in large part by the type of situation that generated the project and whether the goal is improving production skills or mastering a subject. Regardless of the specific project and its emphasis, certain philosophies apply.

In most cases, class productions should emphasize the process of investigating ideas and sharing them through the medium of television. Your projects probably will not be Hollywood quality, but they will reflect learning and your students' first experiences with video.

Grading It? Teach It!

If you are going to grade your students on the quality of their camera work, you owe it to them to teach those skills. If you expect all of your students' shots to be clearly focused, then teach them how to focus a camera. If you're new to video production, read several books on the subject. One of the best teaching tools is a demonstration. Creating a project of your own will reveal to you the skill and time that each project requires and will show your students an example of a project that meets the class requirements.

Talk About Grading

Before the first camcorder begins to roll, talk to your students about the requirements of the project. Let the students know exactly what is expected of them and what they need to do to get the grade they want. Remember, your own attitude will be reflected in the students' finished projects. A fun-and-games approach will probably yield projects that are cute but don't achieve the objectives.

Video Is Subjective

By nature, video production relies on emotions and feelings. As you evaluate student projects, remind yourself that no two people see the same television program exactly the same way.

Set a Timeline and Give Work-in-Progress Grades

Most video projects take a week or more for the class to complete. Establish a reasonable due date and be flexible if most of your students have not finished by this date. Plan several evaluations for each project, not just a final grade based on the finished video. In-progress grades could be given after each step: planning, scriptwriting, shooting the raw footage, and audio dubbing.

Recognize Student Effort

Because many students will be making their first video productions, carefully evaluate student effort as well as the end result. Also, beware of the "same grade for all group members" policy that hides under the deceptive cloak of encouraging teamwork. Be prepared to give different grades to each student in a production group.

Don't Overemphasize Technical Aspects

This philosophy is especially for content-oriented instructors. Be prepared to overlook technical glitches in students' projects. Instead of noting that every shot is out of focus, concentrate on the ideas and effort the video reflects.

Criteria for Grading Video Projects

Consider the following four criteria when assigning grades to video projects, keeping in mind the philosophies underlying them and the different needs of various classroom situations.

Fulfillment of Requirements
- Does the project present the information that you requested? Is the information clearly stated? Does the viewer easily understand the ideas?

Understanding the Content Area
- Does the viewer get the impression that the producers understand and appreciate the content area? Is the program complete in its presentation?

Writing
- Because writing is taught in all elementary and middle school grades, feel comfortable in grading sentence structure, word choice, verb tense, and so forth. Consider the student's writing level as you grade the writing.

Creativity
- Have the students thought of new ways to present the information? Is the enthusiasm of the production team evident in the program?

REMEMBER: Viewing and grading the program should be the natural conclusion to productive class time. Students need guidance and instruction throughout the production process.

Summary

Video production activities can create excitement in the classroom, motivate students, and teach skills that may inspire students to consider a future in communications. As you read through the projects in this book, try to imagine using them in your classroom. With a basic knowledge of simple production equipment and techniques, both students and teachers can benefit from creating video projects. ■

Chapter 2

Managing an Elementary/Middle School Video Production Program

Here's a challenge. Approach 10 fellow educators—teachers, administrators, curriculum resource teachers, media specialists, counselors—and tell them that you will be working with video production this year. Ask them what *they* think this means. You'll probably get 10 different responses. Because video production is still quite new in most elementary and middle schools, very few educators have a firm concept of just what it involves. And, because so many media educators take different approaches to video production, any number of definitions can be correct.

Rather than tell you how video production in schools *should* be, this chapter offers several questions to consider and describes the experiences of several elementary and middle school video production teachers. This way, you can learn from your peers and develop your own ideas about video production. It's a lot like a meeting at the school district office, without the metal folding chairs.

Planning to Manage

Managing your school video production facility is probably one of the most difficult aspects of managing the overall video program. The seat-of-the-pants, best-for-the-kids approach that works so well in the library media center doesn't pass muster when you're trying to supervise 20 nine-year-olds and two camcorders. Neither does a rigid "one size fits all" approach work. To get a handle on video production facility management, consider the following issues. There are no right answers. The best answers are those that work best for you. Considering these issues now (without the 20 nine-year-olds tugging at your sleeve) will prove more fruitful than making decisions in crises.

Access
- Consider how teachers, students, and parents will be given access to the equipment.
- If you encourage video projects and 10 teachers decide to take you up on it, do you have enough equipment for each class? Consider scheduling.
- Will all students in the school have access to the equipment or just the students who are enrolled in video production class?

- Do you plan to circulate (check out) video equipment overnight to teachers? To students?
- Is there a room where teachers and students can work on production? Is the room available before and after school?

Education

- Will you offer a video production course to students? How many weeks will the course last?
- Must teachers complete training before using the equipment? If so, how and when will this training be provided?
- Do you feel comfortable with your level of video expertise?
- What role will your media assistant play in video production?

Basic Rules

- Will food and drink be allowed in the production room?
- How will you ensure students have the proper respect for equipment?
- How will you inform faculty, staff, and students about copyright law?

Role of the Media Specialist

- How do you view your role as a video production instructor?
- Do you expect continuous direct supervision of students who are operating video production equipment? Who will supervise them?
- How much production will *you* undertake? Will you produce school videos, or will you facilitate coworkers' projects?

The intent of these questions is to help you plan for situations or issues you will face when working with video production in schools. Here's an example of a typical situation involving a number of issues covered in the preceding list:

 EXAMPLE

You are a middle school media specialist. During first period, you work with 20 students in your video production class. You guide them through production of a daily news program, assign interview projects, and teach the concepts of television production. One day after the conclusion of the news show, a student who is not enrolled in your class enters the production studio. She says, "I'm in Ms Dozier's advanced English class, and we have to do an independent study project. I've decided to make my own music video."

How do you proceed? There are several questions to consider:

- Do you have extra equipment she can use?
- What video skills (if any) does she have?
- Do you have time to teach her how to use the equipment?
- Do you assign a few of your students to work with her on this project?
- Can your simple studio achieve the level of sophistication that she desires?

Unfortunately, there are no clear-cut answers to these questions. But these types of situations arise in all school video programs. (Consider them signs of the program's success!) Once again, the lesson is to be prepared, to think about management issues before they confront you. Managing a video production facility involves providing service, education, and access while maintaining the integrity of your overall school library media program.

Voices of Experience

The teachers and media specialists featured in this section come from diverse backgrounds and have various levels of experience. However, all work with video production in schools, all love working with kids, and all have something to share.

Michelle Funnell

Citrus Elementary School
Vero Beach, Florida

"Video production in schools provides the opportunity to develop an awareness and appreciation of the procedures of putting video and movies together. The children learn to work as a team to produce an end product."

Under the direction of media specialist Michelle Funnell, students at Citrus Elementary School in Vero Beach, Florida, create a daily morning school news program and tapes about kindergarten readiness for incoming parents. Michelle and her students also videotape most school activities and events.

The Citrus Elementary facility includes a camcorder and a studio camera with tripods, video and audio mixers, and a Panasonic editing system. The students use an Apple computer to create graphics. The school continues to add equipment as funding becomes available.

Michelle strives to include each student in some aspect of the video production. A core team of 20 fifth-graders makes up the regular video crew, which has been selected by a committee of teachers and administrators based on students' written applications. The students meet before school, after school, and during free school time.

Student knowledge of video production concepts is the main objective of Citrus Elementary's video production efforts. Michelle hopes her students will use the knowledge they gained at the elementary level as they go through middle school and high school—and perhaps even choose a career in video production.

Michelle received the Golden Apple award from the Indian River County School Board for her accomplishments in guiding the Citrus Elementary students in video production. ■

Michelle offers this advice to teachers and media specialists working in video production: "Relax. You do not need to know it all at once. You will learn by doing. I have learned something new every day. If all else fails, ask a kid!"

Alice Lawson

Bluewater Elementary School
Niceville, Florida

"As a media educator, I use the process of media production to build teamwork and skills in writing and public speaking. Introduction to media reaches for exposure through hands-on experiences with video equipment, rather than always attempting that polished final product."

Alice Lawson, media specialist at Bluewater Elementary, guides her students through production of a daily news show, KNN—Kids News Network. Alice and her students have also produced a number of community projects, including

- *Our Home/Planet Earth*, a series of public service announcements with an environmental theme;

- *Treasure Trunk*, which featured fourth-graders interviewing local craftpersons;

- *Bridges*, which chronicled the construction of north Florida's Mid-Bay Bridge; and

- *Banks—The Money Movers*, a fourth-grade production about the banking industry.

Bridges won first place in the state media festival.

Bluewater Elementary students use camcorders, two studio cameras with tripods, a Panasonic editing system, a Videonics titler, and a JVC video switcher to create their projects.

All 160 fifth-graders are involved in media production. Each student spends three weeks on the KNN news team. During the first week of school, Alice teaches nine students how to produce the news show. Then, as their three-week stint comes to a close, these students train their replacements. This student-to-student training continues throughout the school year, allowing Alice to help individual students fine-tune their video production techniques. Exposing as many children as possible to the opportunities of media production is Alice's main objective.

> Alice's advice to media educators: "Rotate your news team as often as possible, so many students can participate in media production. I prefer a live broadcast to eliminate the time needed to edit. Some of our favorite shows are the bloopers."

To train students in basic video production techniques, Alice sends each student with a camcorder to videotape several random scenes of a school event. Then, students return to the media center to watch the footage, write a script, and audio dub the tape.

Alice learns most of her video production techniques through first-hand experience. "Quite often," she says, "I discover ideas from the students. I concentrate on building the students' self-esteem and confidence in learning new skills, rather than perfecting a polished product." ∎

Kathy Little

Photo by Gloria Bentley

Shalimar Elementary School
Shalimar, Florida

"Some students never get a chance to do something special. This is why I try to involve as many students as possible in our news show. You never know—you may find a star!"

True to her philosophy, Kathy Little gives every student at Shalimar Elementary School a chance to work on the school news show, which is aired three times each week. Kindergartners, first-graders, and second-graders hold the flag and lead the pledge of allegiance. Third-graders offer a Tip of the Week. Fourth-graders provide trivia questions, book talks, art projects, and environmental news. Fifth-graders serve as directors, camera operators, computer operators, and have the option to anchor the show for a two-week period.

Kathy advises all elementary media specialists to get involved in video production. "Start out, even if you have only one camera," she says. "Add equipment as you can. Try to get teachers involved and excited about production."

In addition to the news show, Kathy and her Shalimar students produce commercials for the school book fair, kindergarten orientation tapes, promotions for the school open house, and messages from the principal. The school video production facility includes two camcorders with tripod dollies, a Panasonic A/V mixer, a separate audio mixer with microphones, and an Amiga computer.

Kathy has two goals for the video production program at Shalimar Elementary School: student self-confidence and knowledge of equipment. Most fifth-graders who are selected to work in video for the entire year learn to operate every item of equipment at the school.

That approach leads to many lessons learned the hard way, and Kathy remembers several humorous episodes. The kindergartner who picked his nose while leading the pledge quickly comes to mind. Kathy also recalls playing the videotape with the national anthem, only to find *The Dating Game* on the tape instead! The unpredictability of doing a live news show keeps the atmosphere exciting and invigorating. ∎

Sharon Shirey

Oak Hill Elementary School
Eglin Air Force Base, Florida

"The skills learned and abilities enhanced through video production are beneficial to all children. Therefore, we strive to involve as many children as possible in an introductory way as opposed to building a high level of skill in a few students."

Oak Hill Elementary, located on Eglin Air Force Base in northwest Florida, is quite active in video production. In addition to producing a news show three times each week, media specialist Sharon Shirey and her students produce *The Oak Hill Connection*, a news show for parents and students, as well as school public relations programs, contest entries, and school orientation tapes. Although there is no formal production class, during the course of the year almost all of the students at Oak Hill are involved in some aspect of video production. Many students who work on the news shows are recommend by their teachers. The students at Oak Hill Elementary work with camcorders, a Panasonic A/V mixer, a Panasonic editing system, a Videonics titler, and an audio mixer with CD player.

Sharon's advice to educators working with video production: "Begin early. Allow twice as much time for a project as you think it may take." At Oak Hill Elementary School, Sharon and her students are always working on that next video project.

Oak Hill Elementary students have won several awards during Sharon's four-year tenure at the school, including two National Awards for Excellence from the Association for Educational Communications Technology (AECT). Sharon's objectives for her students include increased self-confidence, improved communication skills, and the ability to work together as a team. ■

Pattie Smith

Howard Middle School
Orlando, Florida

"Television is a medium that allows students to expand their creativity in the school curriculum."

In addition to her duties as library media specialist, Pattie Smith coordinates the extensive television production program at Howard Middle School. Under Pattie's direction the students produce a news show that includes special reports about school topics. The students also create classroom projects and contest entries.

Her advice for fellow middle school media instructors: "Make sure that you have enough equipment for your class size. Select motivated, responsible students. Establish criteria for selecting students for your video program."

Panasonic has awarded Howard Middle School a grant that allows the school to participate in the Panasonic Kid Witness News Program. Panasonic provides camcorders, editing VCRs, and monitors to the school. In return, students agree to enter biannual video contests sponsored by Panasonic. Recently, the Howard Middle School students won the technical division of the national contest with a video about litter. A student who worked on the project, the student's parents, and Pattie were awarded a trip to New York to receive the award.

Pattie works with 75–100 students per year on a rotating semester basis. The students learn about video production, as well as other forms of media production, while serving as media center assistants. Teachers can also receive training in video production.

Pattie wants students involved in her program to gain a better understanding of using video equipment individually and as a group. ■

Jan Weber

Roy Allen Elementary School
Melbourne, Florida

"Video production is a magical tool to open every child's imagination."

When everyone else was happy with filmstrips and record players, Jan Weber was making videotape at Roy Allen Elementary School in Melbourne, Florida. Jan, who has worked at the school for 18 years, used black-and-white, open-reel videotape to record school events. Now, Jan and her students use three modern camcorders, a Videonics video mixer, and a Radio Shack audio system. Jan teaches three video production classes with a total of about 80 students.

Jan's advice to her fellow media educators is "Start simple and small. Begin each project six weeks *before* you really think you should start."

The school's teachers learned about video production by attending a one-day in-service provided by a video production teacher in a neighboring county. After that in-service, the Roy Allen Elementary teachers began using video as an instructional medium. An alternative education class created a project on life science, and the parent response was quite enthusiastic. Jan reports, "The parents went crazy!" A second-grade class videotaped their trip to the zoo. Jan's objectives for her video production students are simple: knowledge of and love for video production. ■

Summary

Sharing ideas, information, and experiences with other media specialists and television production teachers is important for professional development and invigoration. Perhaps reading about the experiences of these six teachers has provided a new idea or a moment of inspiration. The same results can be garnered by attending local, state, and national media conferences. Formal sessions and information get-togethers can help establish valuable contacts. Many media specialists feel they work in a vacuum, because they are the only media professionals in their school. Going to conferences helps fill that vacuum with a network of new friends.

Whether you have a full production studio or a few camcorders, work with students to create simple video projects. The media specialists featured in this chapter agree that video is a valuable experience for children. ■

Chapter 3

Communicating with Parents

As with all educational endeavors, the success of a school-based video production program depends on parental support. Parents can provide the encouragement their sons and daughters need to be successful. Along with this encouragement, parents can also provide several valuable services.

Parent Resources

Parents of most of the children involved in video production projects at your school can contribute to the success of your program.

Parent volunteers can *supervise students* who wish to shoot at locations outside the classroom. For example, a group of fifth-graders may want to interview the cafeteria manager about the nutritional value in today's menu items. A parent volunteer could accompany the student group, answering any questions about equipment operation, offering advice when needed, and making sure the group stays focused on the task.

Parent volunteers could also *help manage extra student work stations* in the classroom. If a teacher is using three macro lens set-ups at a time, parent volunteers could supervise each of the stations, freeing the teacher to answer content questions and work with the rest of the class.

Providing appropriate paperwork is completed, parents could also *provide transportation* to field trips and remote locations for videotaping student projects. For example, students who have recently studied the weather could interview the weather anchor at the local television station. A team of three or four students, escorted by a parent volunteer, could travel to the station to conduct the interview.

Parents are an excellent *resource for information about careers and hobbies*. Parents can act as interview subjects, facilitate other interviews, and provide insight that will enrich the classroom experience. Many of the projects that follow this chapter rely on adults sharing information with children.

Finally, parents can provide *financial support* to a television production program. Parents whose children have created video projects at school will be more likely to encourage fellow PTA members to fund future video equipment purchases. Also, many parents work for businesses that will donate blank tape, headphones, or tripods.

Forms for Parent–Teacher Communication

School–parent communication often takes the form of a letter or note sent home advising the parents of a school activity and requesting feedback. Figures 3.1–3.10 are several forms that may be useful in school television production activities. Adopt, adapt, or duplicate each form.

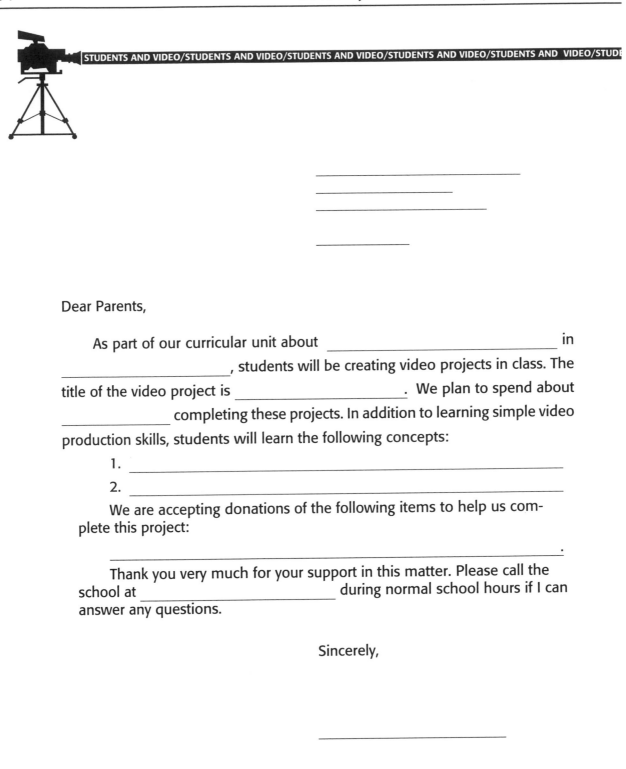

Dear Parents,

As part of our curricular unit about _____ in _____, students will be creating video projects in class. The title of the video project is _____. We plan to spend about _____ completing these projects. In addition to learning simple video production skills, students will learn the following concepts:

1. _____

2. _____

We are accepting donations of the following items to help us complete this project:

_____.

Thank you very much for your support in this matter. Please call the school at _____ during normal school hours if I can answer any questions.

Sincerely,

_____

Fig. 3.1   Letter to introduce video production activities in the classroom.

STUDENTS AND VIDEO/STUDENTS AND VIDEO/STUDENTS AND VIDEO/STUDENTS AND VIDEO/STUDENTS AND VIDEO/STUDE

Polk Avenue Elementary School
9495 Smith Lane
Anytown, State 12345

April 17, 1995

Dear Parents,

As part of our curricular unit about   Food and Nutrition   in my fourth-grade class , students will be creating video projects in class. The title of the video project is   "Making a Healthy Lunch."   We plan to spend about   one week   completing these projects. In addition to learning simple video production skills, students will learn the following concepts:

1. Basic nutritional information, including food groups and serving sizes
2. How to plan a nutritious meal

We are accepting donations of the following items to help us complete this project:

                    Blank VHS videotape, paper plates   .

Thank you very much for your support in this matter. Please call the school at 987-6543, extension 123 during normal school hours if I can answer any questions.

Sincerely,

Ms Nancy Hobbs

Fig. 3.2 Completed form letter to introduce video production activities in the classroom.

Parent Survey

Dear Parent,

Throughout the year, we will be integrating simple video production skills into our regular school curriculum. We believe that this approach will increase student interest in class work and involve the students as active learners. Please complete the following survey and return it to school as soon as possible. Thank you.

_____
Name

— — — — — — — — — — — — — — — — —

Student name _____

Parent name _____

Phone number (home)_____

Phone number (work)_____

Is there a television in the child's home?	Yes	No
Is there a videocassette recorder (VCR) in the child's home?	Yes	No
Does your child know the basic operation of the television and VCR?	Yes	No
Does your child have access to a camcorder?	Yes	No

If so, what format? (circle one)
       VHS   VHS-C   8mm   Hi8mm   Other_____

Does your child know how to operate the camcorder?	Yes	No
Would you allow your child to use the camcorder at home to complete school projects?	Yes	No
Would you be interested in volunteering in the classroom as we create our video projects?	Yes	No

Questions/Comments: _____

_____

Fig. 3.3   Parent survey.

STUDENTS AND VIDEO/STUDENTS AND VIDEO/STUDENTS AND VIDEO/STUDENTS AND VIDEO/STUDENTS AND VIDEO/STUD

Permission for Checking Out
Video Production Equipment

Students creating video projects in school frequently want to use the school's video production equipment off-campus and after school to create class projects. Although this practice is not required and in no way affects the student grade, the school makes a camcorder available for student check-out with parental permission.

Because of the delicate nature of video production equipment, the limited supply of equipment at the school, and the price of repairing and replacing the equipment, _____ School requires parental permission and acceptance of the following terms before equipment can be checked out to students for off-campus use.

1. I give permission for my child _____ to check out equipment from _____ School.

2. I agree to pay for repair of equipment if it becomes damaged during the check-out period. If the equipment is lost or stolen, I agree to pay its fair replacement value. Payment will be due immediately and is *not* contingent upon any insurance payments or decisions.

3. I will encourage my child to use the equipment safely and responsibly.

4. I understand that my child should videotape only school-related projects with this equipment.

5. I agree to provide for the return of this equipment to school by _____ a.m. on the next school day. The equipment must be returned even if the student is unable to attend school the next day. I understand that I am responsible for the equipment until it is returned to the teacher, media specialist, or designee.

6. If I have any questions or concerns, I will notify the school *before* the proposed check-out day.

7. Phone contact with the parent is required the day of each check-out.

_____

Parent or guardian signature

_____   _____

Home phone   Work phone

Fig. 3.4 Equipment check-out form.

Parent Interest and Career Survey

Dear Parent,

As your daughter or son may have mentioned, we are using video production techniques this year in many aspects of our curriculum. We are always interested in our students' parents as a resource for possible interview and program topics. As we begin a list of these topics, we hope you will help us by telling us about your hobbies, interests, and careers.

Parent name _____

Child's name _____

Phone number _____   Best time to call _____

What jobs or careers have you had or do you have that you could share with the children?

_____

_____

What hobbies, interests, or activities would you be willing to share with the children?

_____

_____

_____

What places have you lived in or visited that you would be willing to talk about to the children?

_____

_____

_____

Thank you for taking the time to complete this survey. We appreciate your interest!

Fig. 3.5   Parent interest and career survey.

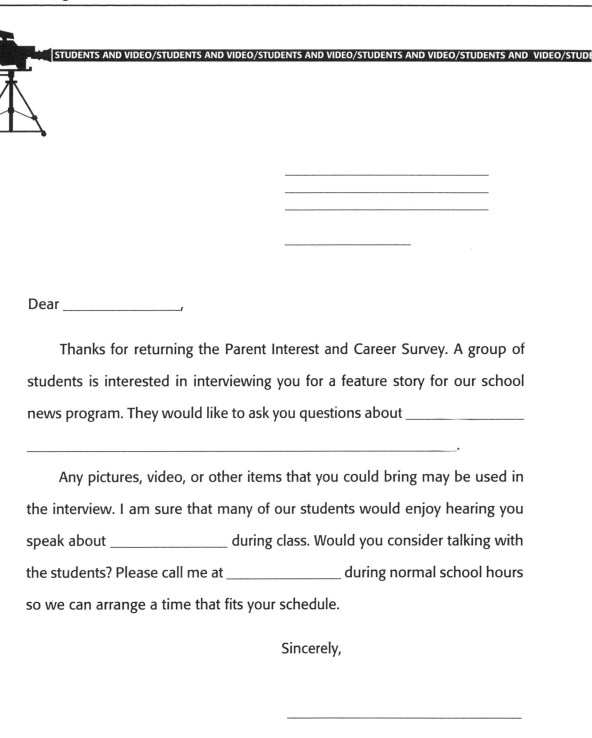

STUDENTS AND VIDEO/STUDENTS AND VIDEO/STUDENTS AND VIDEO/STUDENTS AND VIDEO/STUDENTS AND VIDEO/STUDE

Dear _____,

Thanks for returning the Parent Interest and Career Survey. A group of students is interested in interviewing you for a feature story for our school news program. They would like to ask you questions about _____ _____.

Any pictures, video, or other items that you could bring may be used in the interview. I am sure that many of our students would enjoy hearing you speak about _____ during class. Would you consider talking with the students? Please call me at _____ during normal school hours so we can arrange a time that fits your schedule.

Sincerely,

_____

Fig. 3.6   Request for parent interview or visit.

Lincoln Elementary School
1234 Illinois Lane
Anytown, State 12345

May 15, 1996

Dear _____ Mr. Christopher _____ ,

Thanks so much for returning the Parent Interest and Career Survey. A group of students is interested in interviewing you for a feature story for our school news program. They would like to ask you questions about ___ your ___ recent trip to Alaska, including your fishing experiences ___ .

Any pictures, video, or other items that you could bring may be used in the interview. I am sure that many of our students would enjoy hearing you speak about ___ Alaska ___ during class. Would you consider talking with the students? Please call me at ___ 123-4567 ___ during normal school hours so we can arrange a time that fits your schedule.

Sincerely,

Ms Nancy Hobbs

Fig. 3.7   Sample request for parent interview or visit.

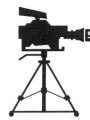

STUDENTS AND VIDEO/STUDENTS AND VIDEO/STUDENTS AND VIDEO/STUDENTS AND VIDEO/STUDENTS AND VIDEO/STUD

Home Video Alert!

Dear Parents,

We are using video production techniques this year. Frequently, students ask about previously recorded video to use in their projects. Do you have any videotapes you have recorded that you would be willing to share with our class? If so, please list the topics and format (8mm, VHS, etc.) below. Thank you.

Topic	**Format**

Fig.3.8 Request for video footage.

Home Video Alert!

Dear Parents,

We are using video production techniques this year. Frequently, students ask about previously recorded video to use in their projects. Do you have any videotapes you have recorded that you would be willing to share with our class? If so, please list the topics and format (8mm, VHS, etc.) below. Thank you.

Topic	**Format**
Vacation to Niagara Falls	VHS
Vacation to Disneyworld	VHS-C
Florida Caverns State Park	VHS
Softball game	VHS
Birthday party	VHS

Fig. 3.9 Sample response to request for video footage.

Calling All Field Trip Chaperones!

Dear Parents,

The _____ of _____

is planning a field trip to _____. On this trip, we plan to learn about

_____.

The planned date of this field trip is _____.

We are recruiting chaperones for this field trip. The school bus will leave

our school at _____ and we should return to school by

_____. Would you be interested in chaperoning this field

trip? If so, please return the bottom half of this form to school as soon as

possible. Thank you.

Sincerely,

_____

= =

Yes, I am interested in serving as a field trip chaperon.

_____   _____
Name   Student name

_____   _____
Phone number   Best time to call

Fig. 3.10   Request for chaperone.

Social Development
pages 44–60

Social Studies
pages 61–65

Language Arts
pages 66–74

Science
pages 75–81

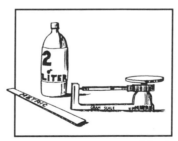

Math
pages 82–87

Safety and Health
pages 88–97

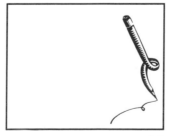

Physical Education
pages 98–104

Art
pages 105–108

School and Community
pages 109–118

<u>P</u>roject Plan
Meet My Friend

Objective

Students will learn to conduct an on-camera interview with one of their friends.

Equipment

- Video camera
- Tripod
- Microphone
- Headphones (to check microphone sound)

Procedure

1. Discuss with your class the use of interviews as a way of introducing someone to an audience. Emphasize the three basic components of an interview:

   Introduction: Name of guest and some brief comment about the guest.

   Questions: Should be used to allow the guest to share information with the audience. Stress the use of open-ended questions rather than questions that require a one-word response.
   - Wrong: Do you play baseball?
   - Right: What do you like most about playing baseball?

   Closing: Thank the guest and summarize one or two aspects of the interview.

2. Distribute the Video Project: Meet My Friend form to students. You can pair up the students or each student may select an interviewee.

3. Have some students role-play their interviews in front of the class before videotaping. Students can practice the aspects of good interviewing, such as eye contact, microphone position, and camera presence. You can even videotape some of the practice interviews to critique.

4. Have students videotape the interviews.

Extension Activities

1. Watch some professional interviews of sports figures, entertainment stars, or local officials.

2. Invite a reporter from your local news station to speak to the class about interviewing. You could even interview this person on camera. The reporter could help critique your interviews!

3. Allow students to look through some magazines (for example, *People, Time, TV Guide, Teen,* or *Sports Illustrated*) for famous people they would like to interview. Have students write an introduction and some questions they would ask their guest. Have each student cut out a picture of the interviewee, paste the picture on paper, and write the introduction and questions on the paper below the picture.

Video Project
Meet My Friend

1. What is your friend's name?

First _____

Last _____

2. List some sports or hobbies your friend likes to do.

_____

_____

_____

3. Does your friend have any special talents, like singing, dancing, or drawing?

_____

_____

_____

4. What are two of your friend's favorite things to do or places to go on weekends or during vacations?

_____

_____

_____

5. What does your friend want to be when she or he grows up?

_____

_____

_____

Introducing Your Friend

Use some of the information you found out about your friend to write an introduction for your interview.

Hello. ... Today I would like you to meet my friend, _____ .
(friend's name)

[He/She] enjoys _____
(hobby or sport)

and also likes to _____ .
(talent)

Interviewing Your Friend

Write down three questions you could ask your friend. Try to ask open-ended questions that need more than one or two words to answer.

Question 1 _____

_____

Question 2 _____

_____

Question 3 _____

_____

Tell your friend what questions you are going to ask so your friend can think about what to say.

Ending Your Interview

It is important to let your guest and your audience know that the interview is ending. You should thank your guest and say something about what you have learned from your interview.

Thank you, _____ , for joining us
(friend's name)

on our show today. We enjoyed hearing about _____ .
(activity/sport/hobby)

For _____ , this has been
(name of show)

_____ .
(your name)

Videotape your interview. Share the tape with your classmates.

Social Development

P roject Plan
My Pet

Objective
Students will write/produce a short video about their home or classroom pet.

Equipment
- Video camera
- Audio mixer
- Music source (tape deck, CD player, phonograph)
- Microphone
- Tripod

Procedure
Instructions for audio dubbing appear on pages 17–20.

1. Initiate discussion about home or classroom pets, their care, and supplies needed to care for them.
2. Distribute the Video Project: My Pet form. Have students complete the form.
3. Have students use the information from their My Pet forms to write six to eight sentences. This will be the script for the project.
4. Have students videotape footage using camera shots listed on their My Pet forms.
5. Have students audio dub their scripts over their videotaped footage.

Extension Activities
1. Have students check out books from the school or local library about pets and the care of pets. Create a classroom display.
2. Invite a local veterinarian to the classroom to speak about the care of pets.
3. Plan a field trip to a local pet store to speak to the merchant about pets and pet supplies.

Video Project
My Pet

1. What kind of pet do you have? _____

2. What is its name? _____

3. List the things you need to take care of your pet.

   _____

   _____

   _____

   _____

   _____

4. Is there anything special about your pet that people might like to know? What?

   _____

   _____

   _____

5. Write a story about your pet using all the information on this paper. This will be your script.

   _____

   _____

   _____

   _____

   _____

   _____

   _____

   _____

6. List six camera shots you would need to make a video about your pet.

1. _____

2. _____

3. _____

4. _____

5. _____

6. _____

7. Videotape your pet, using the camera shots you listed above.

8. Practice reading your script while you watch the videotape. Then audio dub your script on the videotape.

Social Development

Project Plan
Growing Up!

Objective

Students will produce a short video using photographs of themselves.

Equipment

- Student photos
- Video camera
- Tripod
- Monitor
- Audio mixer
- Music source (tape deck, CD player, phonograph)

Procedure

Detailed instructions for making macro projects, including title cards, appear on pages 12–17. Instructions for audio dubbing appear on pages 17–20.

1. Have the students bring in 12–15 photographs of themselves, beginning with one or two baby photos and ending with a current photo.

2. Help students number the photos in chronological order on the back of each photo, with number 1 being the oldest photo (that is, when student was youngest), and the last photo being the most current.

3. Have each student create a title card. Title cards can be made using 6-×-8-inch index cards, 3-×-5-inch cards trimmed to 3 by 4 inches, posterboard, or a character generator.

4. Videotape the photos. Students' projects can be enhanced if the student can fade-in on the title card and fade-out on the last photo.

5. Audio dub music on the videotaped footage.

Extension Activities

1. Create a Guess Who? bulletin board display using students' baby pictures.

2. Invite other teachers and school workers to bring in photos of themselves as young children. Macro each picture and then videotape the teacher or school worker on the job. Students will have fun matching the baby photos with the adults.

3. Many baby animals look quite different from their adult counterparts. Tadpoles turn into frogs, and caterpillars become butterflies. Students can read about animal changes, then write essays or draw pictures comparing animals as babies and as adults.

Video Project
Growing Up!

1. Collect pictures of yourself growing up. You will need about 12–15 photographs. Try to have one or two baby pictures. One photo should be of you as you are now.

2. Number the pictures on the backs of each picture in order by the date the picture was taken. Number 1 should be the oldest picture of you and the last photo should be the most recent photo of you.

3. Create a title for your project. Use an index card to create a colorful title card.

4. Videotape the title card and your photos. Try using a fade-in for your title card and a fade-out for your last photo.

5. Audio dub music on your tape. Fade the music after your last photo.

6. Share your project with your friends and family.

Social Development

Project Plan
My Family

Objective

Students will produce a short video about their family.

Equipment

- Photographs of family and family members
- Video camera
- Tripod
- Audio mixer
- Music source (tape deck, CD player, phonograph)
- Microphone

Procedure

Detailed instructions for making macro projects, including title cards, appear on pages 12–17. Instructions for audio dubbing appear on pages 17–20.

1. Initiate discussion about the people that make up a family. Students may draw or paint a picture of their family to begin the discussion. These pictures could be used as the title page for the project.

2. Distribute the Video Project: My Family form.

3. Allow the students to complete the My Family form. This sheet may be taken home so parents can help students answer the questions and select photographs.

4. Students should photograph *only* those pictures needed to complete the project.

5. Once students have collected all the pictures needed for completing this project, they may videotape the pictures. (See the section on Macro Projects.)

6. Students can audio dub their script onto their videotape. Have them practice reading their script once or twice as they watch their videotape before they actually audio dub the videotape.

Extension Activities

1. Have the students bring in photos of their families on vacation or doing recreational activities. Create a bulletin board display using these photos. Students may enjoy picking up postcards or brochures advertising some of the places pictured in the display. These materials can be added to the display.

2. All families are different. Select some books about families to read with your class or to place in a reading center.

VIdeo Project
My Family

1. List the names of the people in your family and their relationship to you.

   Example: John—brother
   Lisa—sister
   Diane—mother

   _____

   _____

   _____

   _____

   _____

2. What are some activities the people in your family like to do?

   Example: Mother likes to work in the garden.

   _____

   _____

   _____

   _____

   _____

   _____

3. Write about something your family likes to do together. It could be a place to visit or an activity.

   Examples: The beach, going on a picnic.

   _____

   _____

   _____

4. What is the title of your video project? Make a title card.

_____

_____

5. You will need to have the following photos for your project:

Photo	Have One	Need One
A picture of your family	_____	_____
A picture of each family member doing something they enjoy	_____	_____
Things your family likes to do together	_____	_____

6. Use the information in this project to write a script about your family.

7. Videotape your title and photos. Record each picture for 10 seconds.

8. Rehearse your script while you watch the videotape. Audio dub your script on the videotape.

Social Development

Project Plan
My Neighborhood

Objective

Students will write and produce a short video project about their neighborhood.

Equipment

- Video camera
- Tripod
- Audio mixer
- Music source (tape deck, CD player, phonograph)
- Microphone

Procedure

Instructions for audio dubbing appear on pages 17–20.

1. Initiate a discussion about neighborhoods. Hang up a local street map and have students place a marker on the street where they live.

2. Distribute the Video Project: My Neighborhood form. Have students complete the information on the form.

3. Have students use the information from the My Neighborhood form to write a short paragraph about their neighborhood. This will be their script for this project.

4. Have students videotape the necessary footage for the project.

5. Have students audio dub their script on the video footage.

Extension Activity

1. Obtain some old aerial photographs to show students what the area looked like before their neighborhoods were built.

Video Project
My Neighborhood

1. What is the name of your neighborhood or the name of your street?

_____

_____

2. Describe your house.

_____

_____

_____

_____

3. What are some fun things to do in your neighborhood?

_____

_____

_____

_____

_____

4. Is there anything special about your neighborhood that people might like to know?

_____

_____

_____

_____

5. Use the information on this paper to write a script about your neighborhood.

6. List six camera shots you need for a video project about your neighborhood.

1. _____

2. _____

3. _____

4. _____

5. _____

6. _____

7. Videotape your neighborhood, using the camera shots you listed above.

8. Practice reading your script while you watch the videotape. Then audio dub your script on the videotape.

Social Development

Project Plan:
Parents at Work

Objective

Students will conduct an interview with their parent about their parent's job and workplace.

Equipment

- Video camera
- Tripod
- Microphone
- Headphone (to check microphone sound)

Procedure

1. Initiate discussion about jobs, training, and job skills. A good starting point may be your job as a teacher. Discuss the training, skills, and some of the tasks you perform as a teacher. Ask students about their parents and their parents' workplaces.

2. Distribute the Project Plan: Parents at Work form. Read over the form and discuss it with the class. Students will probably need to take this form home so their parents can help them complete it.

3. Schedule interview times with parents. (See figures 3.5, 3.6, and 3.7 for form letters to use.)

4. It's a good idea to practice interviewing techniques with students. Set up the video camera and select students to role-play reporters and parents. After the role-play, review the tapes and make suggestions for handling the microphone, making eye contact with the guest or camera, and camera shots.

5. Videotape the parent interviews.

Extension Activities

1. Have parents take photos of their workplaces. Create a bulletin board display with the pictures.

2. Have students write about a job they would like to have when they grow up. Have them research the job to find out about training, education, and skills they need to obtain it.

3. Invite a job counselor to speak to the class about applying for jobs and finding jobs for qualified people.

Video Project
Parents at Work

1. Pick one parent for this project.

Check one: _____ Mother   _____ Father

2. What is your mother's or father's job (occupation)?

_____

3. Where does your parent work (name of company)?

_____

4. What are some of the things your parent does on the job?

_____

_____

_____

_____

_____

5. What does your parent like most about the job?

_____

_____

6. Is there any equipment or tools that your parent needs to know how to use to do the job?

_____

_____

_____

_____

7. What kind of skills or training does someone need to be able to get jobs like your parent?

_____

_____

_____

8. Ask your parent to come to school for an interview about the job. Have your parent wear the clothes they normally wear to work for the interview. Ask your parent to bring a tool or piece of equipment to show during the interview.

9. Interviewing your parent: sample script.

Introduction: Today, we are going to meet _____
                                                                                (parent's name)

who is a _____ . She/he works
                                                    (job title)

at _____ in _____ .
                        (company name)   (city, state)

Questions: Use the information from your video project form to help you write these questions.

    Question 1 _____

    Question 2 _____

    Question 3 _____

Summary: Thank you, _____, for telling us
                                                    (parent's name)

about your job as a _____ . It was nice of you to take the
                                        (job title)

time to come to school for this interview. For _____ , this has been
                                                                        (name of show)

_____ .
            (your name)

Social Studies

Project Plan
_____

*I Want
to Visit _____ !*

Objective

Students will write and produce a macro video project about a country they would like to visit.

Equipment

- Video camera
- Tripod
- Audio mixer
- Music source (tape deck, CD player, phonograph)
- Microphone

Procedure

Detailed instructions for making macro projects, including title cards, appear on pages 12–17. Instructions for audio dubbing appear on pages 17–20.

1. Have students bring in photos or postcards from some of their favorite places they have visited. Discuss things they saw, unique features of that place, and what they enjoyed the most while they were there.

2. Distribute the Video Project: I Want to Visit _____ ! form. Have the students complete the information on the form.

3. Help students locate information and pictures for their video project. Local travel agencies, chambers of commerce, or tourist boards will be glad to supply information for these projects.

4. Set out some materials for making title cards. Have each student create a title card for the project. (See page 15 for instructions.)

5. Have students videotape the title card and photographs.

6. Have students audio dub their script over the videotaped footage.

Extension Activities

1. Send home a note about the planned activity. Ask if parents would like to share photos or slides of their favorite trip with the class.

2. In many countries and regions of the world, unique musical forms have developed, for example, reggae in the Caribbean. Bring in some examples of local music, or ask the music instructor to teach a few simple cultural songs to the class.

3. Visit a travel agency. See how professionals arrange trips for vacation and business travel.

Video Project
I Want to Visit _____ !

1. What country would you like to visit?

_____

2. Use an encyclopedia, atlas, or travel brochure to find out some interesting facts about this country. Here are some of the things you should know about:

Major language or languages spoken:

1. _____

2. _____

Major tourist sites:

1. _____

2. _____

3. _____

4. _____

How would you get there?

1. _____

2. _____

Native animals you would see while there:

1. _____

2. _____

3. _____

4. _____

5. _____

3. Write a story using the facts you have learned. This will be your script for the project.

4. Find pictures (for videotaping) of this country and the places you would like to see. Visit a travel agency, the public library, or write to that country's tourist board to ask for pictures.

5. Make a title card for your project. Be creative.

6. Videotape the title card and photographs.

7. Audio dub your script on the videotape.

Project Plan
Nation Exploration

NOTE: This project may be adapted to fit any age group, but is primarily aimed at middle school classes. Teachers should carefully plan the requirements for this project based on the following project plan and student hand-outs. Some classes may undertake this as a weekly project, while others may use it as a substitute for a research paper.

Objective

Students will write and produce a macro video project based on their research about a country.

Equipment

- Video camera
- Tripod
- Audio mixer
- Music source (tape deck, CD player, phonograph)
- Microphone

Procedure

Detailed instructions for making macro projects, including title cards, appear on pages 12–17. Instructions for audio dubbing appear on pages 17–20.

1. Review the student project plan and determine what information your students should research. (See student handout on the next page.)

2. Place students in groups (or allow them to select their own groups) of two or three students. Assign each group a country for research.

3. Distribute the Project Plan: Nation Exploration form. Tell the students which items of information you want them to find. They can mark these items on their project plans.

4. Allow students to use several days of class time to find the information. Visits to the media center and a classroom multimedia computer are especially helpful. If you are requiring students to draw maps, provide tracing paper and allow students to photocopy their map template for all their maps. Provide colored pencils, markers, scissors, glue and construction paper.

5. For videotaping instructions, refer to pages 15–17. Allow students enough time to complete their videotaping and audio dub.

Extension Activities

1. Ask students to tell about the music they used in their project. What instruments were used? Why were those instruments developed in that country? Students can investigate the instruments in the school library media center.

2. Survey parents, faculty, and community members to determine if someone who has lived in or visited another country is willing to speak about it to the class.

3. Plan a food day at which students can prepare dishes native to their assigned country and share them with the class. This would add a special touch to the project viewing.

Video Project
Nation Exploration

1. What country are you going to explore?

   _____

2. Check the information that will be included in your project, following your teacher's instructions.

   _____ flag   _____ location map

   _____ government   _____ flag or coat of arms (history)

   _____ transportation used in country   _____ economy (type of business)

   _____ education and literacy rate   _____ population (total, density, growth)

   _____ climate (chart)   _____ physical features (map)

   _____ recreation and entertainment   _____ natural resources

   _____ arts   _____ history (major time periods)

3. Use reference resources (for example, encyclopedia, atlas, almanac, or computer search) to find the information required for this project. Take careful notes as you research. Make sure to note the name and publication date of each source used.

4. Prepare at least one visual for each item that you checked on the list above. Visuals include maps, postcards, photographs, charts, and drawings.

5. Prepare a title card about your country. The title card should tell the audience what country is featured in your report. A second card should include the names of the members of your group.

6. Make a note card listing the references that you used in this project.

7. Write a script for your project. Be sure to include all of the information the teacher asked for.

8. Select music that reflects the culture of your country. Check local libraries and media centers for international music. Many CD-ROM programs contain music from other countries. Community members who have lived or traveled to your subject country may also be able to provide music.

9. Videotape your visuals as a macro project, including the title cards and the reference card. Consult your script to make sure that each visual remains on camera for the appropriate amount of time.

10. Watch the videotape and practice your script. Make any necessary changes to the script.

11. Audio dub your script and music on the videotape.

Language Arts

Project Plan
Another Great Book

Objective

Students will create a video project that tells about a book they have read.

Equipment

- Video camera
- Tripod
- Audio mixer
- Music source (tape deck, CD player, phonograph)
- Microphone

Procedure

Detailed instructions for making macro projects, including title cards, appear on pages 12–17. Instructions for audio dubbing appear on pages 17–20.

1. Discuss with students some great books they have read. What details about a book are important to reveal when you are telling someone about the book? What details do you not tell them?

2. Distribute the Video Project: Another Great Book form. Have students complete the form. You might need to arrange a class visit to the media center to complete this part of the project.

3. Have students use the information to create a script for their project.

4. Have students videotape the necessary footage to complete their project.

   NOTE: This project can be adapted so that the student actually tells about a book on camera rather than videotaping and audio dubbing. In this case, use a lavaliere microphone and have the student hold and display the book while talking about it.

5. Have the students audio dub their script over the videotaped footage.

Extension Activities

1. Ask your media specialist if your class can create a display of their favorite books in the media center.

2. Have the students create surveys to give to students in other classes to find out what are some of their favorite books.

3. Have the students research Newbery– and Caldicott–award winning books from the last five years. What are these awards and how are books selected to receive them?

Video Project
Another Great Book

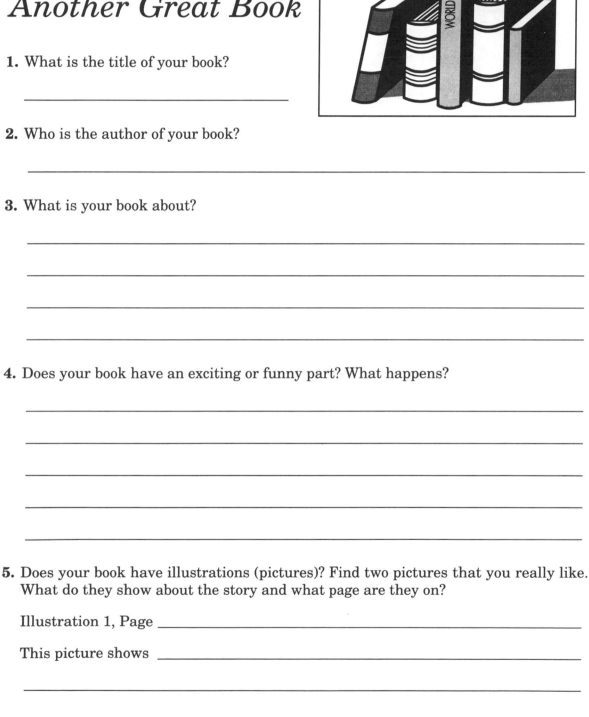

1. What is the title of your book?

_____

2. Who is the author of your book?

_____

3. What is your book about?

_____

_____

_____

_____

4. Does your book have an exciting or funny part? What happens?

_____

_____

_____

_____

_____

5. Does your book have illustrations (pictures)? Find two pictures that you really like. What do they show about the story and what page are they on?

Illustration 1, Page _____

This picture shows _____

_____

_____

Illustration 2, Page _____

This picture shows _____

_____

_____

6. Why would you recommend this book to another student to read?

_____

_____

7. Use this information to write a script about your book.

> *Example:* I read a wonderful book this week that I think you would enjoy. It's *Sylvester and the Magic Pebble*, and it was written by William Steig. In this story, Sylvester finds a magic pebble that grants him whatever he wishes. This seems like a great idea until Sylvester accidently wishes for something silly. The story has a happy ending, and anyone who likes reading about magic and fantasy will really enjoy this book. Look for this book in our school library.

8. List six camera shots you would like to use in your project. Be sure to include the two illustrations.

1. _____

2. _____

3. _____

4. _____

5. _____

6. _____

9. Videotape your project.

10. Audio dub your script on the videotape.

Language Arts

Project Plan

Interviewing Storybook Characters

Objective

The students will videotape an interview with a storybook character.

Equipment

- Video camera
- Tripod
- Microphone

Procedure

1. Initiate discussion about some favorite storybook characters. Allow students to imagine they are interviewing the characters about what happened to them in the stories. What questions would they ask? How would they introduce them? What did the characters learn from their experiences?

2. Distribute the Video Project: Interviewing Storybook Characters form. Review the project with students, discussing possible candidates for their interviews. Students will work in pairs, one being the character and the other being the reporter. Students should work together to complete the project form.

3. Allow students to role play their interviews before taping day. You might videotape these rehearsals to allow students to critique their own performances.

4. Videotape the interviews.

Extension Activities

1. Storybook characters are often used to teach valuable lessons. For example, *The Three Little Pigs* reminds children to work hard and not take short cuts just to save a little work. Have your students make a list of stories and the lessons they teach. This could be made into a display for the classroom or media center.

2. Where do fables come from? Students can research the origins of many famous tales and fables. Who was Hans Christian Andersen? Who were the Grimm Brothers?

Video Project

Interviewing Storybook Characters

Think of a storybook character. Imagine you could interview this character for a news show or talk show. Who would you choose and what would you ask?

Reporter _____

Character _____

1. What storybook character would you like to interview?

_____

2. What does this character look like? Do you need any props? *Example:* For Little Red Riding Hood, you need a red cape and a picnic basket.

_____

_____

_____

3. Write an introduction for your interview.

> *Example:* Standing next to me is Little Red Riding Hood, who just barely escaped from the Big Bad Wolf. She is going to tell us about her narrow escape earlier today.

_____

_____

_____

_____

4. Write three questions you would like to ask your storybook character.

Question 1 _____

Question 2 _____

Question 3 _____

5. Write a summary for your interview.

Example: Well, Little Red Riding Hood, you are certainly lucky you weren't hurt or injured today. Perhaps walking alone in the woods is not a good idea for young children.

Summary _____

_____

_____

_____

_____

This has been _____
(reporter's name)

reporting for _____ .
(show title)

6. Practice your interview several times so you have the introduction and the summary memorized.

7. Tape your interview.

Language Arts

Project Plan

Storytelling in the Classroom

Objective

The students will create and tell a story on videotape.

Equipment

- Video camera
- Tripod
- Microphone

Procedure

1. Motivate the students by telling a story or inviting a local storyteller to the classroom.

2. Discuss with students the aspects of good storytelling: expression, familiarity with the story, sound effects.

3. Distribute the Video Project: Storytelling in the Classroom form. Allow students time to synthesize ideas and complete the form. Also provide time for practice and rehearsal. (Because this can be a noisy project, try holding rehearsals outside during nice weather.)

4. Videotape some of the rehearsals so students can critique their work. Some videotaping tips include:

   - Use a tripod.
   - Set the camera on a bust-shot so the students' facial expressions can be seen. Place the camera at the level of your subject, not too high. Don't film down on students.
   - Use a good microphone. Poor sound quality will detract from the quality of the projects. A lavaliere microphone is suggested so students' hands will be free to gesture. A shotgun microphone could also be used effectively.

5. Videotape the storytellers. Watch them in class!

Extension Activities

1. Professional storytellers reside or work in most cities. They will be glad to come to your class to tell stories and provide advice for your young storytellers.

2. In cultures where writing was absent, storytelling took the place of books in providing information essential for cultural development and everyday living. Have your students research some folktales, legends, or fairy tales to see why they were told as stories before they were written down. Two good sources of folktales are *The Corn Woman: Stories and Legends of the Hispanic Southwest* (Libraries Unlimited, 1994) and *Clever Folk: Tales of Wisdom, Wit and Wonder* (Libraries Unlimited, 1993).

Video Project

Storytelling in the Classroom

Have you ever heard someone tell a really good story? They use lots of expression and details to make the story come alive! Today we're going to tell a story.

1. What is your story about?

_____

_____

_____

2. Who are the characters in your story?

_____

_____

_____

_____

3. Where does the story take place?

_____

4. Storytelling can be even more fun with sound effects! What are some sound effects you need in your story? How can you make them?

Sound effect 1 _____

_____

Sound effect 2 _____

_____

Sound effect 3 _____

_____

Sound effect 4 _____

_____

5. How does the story end?

_____

_____

_____

6. Write a script or outline of your story.

7. Practice telling your story to a friend. Have your friend make the sound effects during the story. You may need to practice your story several times until you both know it completely.

8. Videotape your storytelling. Have your friend make the sound effects off camera.

9. Share your storytelling tape with classmates.

Science

Project Plan
Story of a Seed

Objective
The students will produce a video about the planting, care, and growth of a seed into a plant.

Equipment
- Video camera
- Tripod
- Audio mixer
- Sound source (tape deck, CD player, phonograph)
- Microphone

Procedure
Instructions for audio dubbing appear on pages 17–20.

1. Bring in an assortment of seeds and one or two adult plants. Ask students what they need to do to get the seeds to grow into plants. Discuss materials and care. Then discuss observation techniques.

   Obtain seeds that quickly germinate and grow. Bean seeds are good for this project, but many others grow just as fast. A local merchant can help you obtain fast-growing seeds. Check a local nursery or hardware store.

2. Distribute the Video Project: The Story of a Seed form. Discuss the plan with the students and help them complete the form.

3. Students may do individual videos, but groups can do the project just as easily. Or, this could be a class project. Several shots can be taken of the students as they complete each step in planting and growing their seeds.

4. Bring in the materials to plant and grow the seeds. These should include:
   - seeds
   - soil
   - small containers or pots
   - watering can

5. When videotaping the plant growth, small cards can be placed in front of the plants with the date or Day 1, Day 2, Day 3, and so on.

6. Avoid videotaping extended shots unless you plan on editing the tape. Shots of 5–10 seconds will be long enough for the video.

---

7. After all videotaping is completed, students should preview the footage and write their scripts. They should practice reading the script while watching the footage to make any necessary script changes before audio dubbing.

8. Audio dub music and the script over the videotaped footage.

Extension Activities

1. This activity can be used to teach graphing. Students can chart plants' growth (in centimeters) by days or weeks. Students also can compare the growth rates of various types of plants.

2. Compare the effects of environmental factors on plant growth. For example, what happens when one plant is given only half the amount of sunlight as another plant? What happens if one plant gets only half as much water as another plant? Do different soils affect plants' growth?

Video Project
Story of a Seed

Have you ever planted a seed and watched it grow? Wouldn't it be fun to make a video project about a seed growing into a plant? Follow this simple outline and you can make it happen!

1. What kind of seed will you use?

_____

2. What do you need to plant your seed?

_____

3. What do you do to help your seed grow?

_____

_____

4. How can you tell how fast your seed is growing?

_____

_____

5. Now, use the information above to plan your video. Describe five camera shots you will use.

1. _____

2. _____

3. _____

4. _____

5. _____

6. How will your video end?

_____

As your seed begins to grow, you won't need to videotape every day. Once or twice a week for a few weeks will do.

7. After your video is completed, watch it carefully. Write a short script to go with the video. Use the information on this project to help you write your script!

8. Audio dub your script on the videotape.

Science

Project Plan

What's with the Weather?

Objective

The students will produce a video weather report.

Equipment

- Video camera
- Tripod
- Microphone

Procedure

1. Let students watch some local weather reports. Tape one or two and let students watch them in class. Also, have some copies of the local newspaper on hand so students can use them to look up the weather forecast.

2. Distribute the Video Project: What's With the Weather? form. Discuss some aspects important to include in the weather forecast. How does the weatherperson dress and talk? What kind of weather symbols are used?

3. Decorate a bulletin board, or some other areas to make the background for videotaping the weather forecasts. Students may want to place symbols and temperatures on a map or drawing. Magnets can be attached to the symbols, and these can be placed on a chalkboard. Or tape can be used to stick symbols on a map on a wall or bulletin board.

4. Allow students to practice their weather forecasts. Videotape one or two so students can critique their work.

5. When taping, use a lavaliere or shotgun microphone. The weather forecasters need to use their hands to point to or place symbols on the map.

Extension Activities

1. Invite a local weather forecaster to speak to your class.

2. Plan a visit to a local news station to see how the weather forecast is prepared and videotaped. Students will be surprised to see the weather forecaster is not really standing in front of the maps. These are keyed in electronically; the forecaster stands in front of a green/blue screen.

3. Set up a rain gauge outside your school. Have students record the amount of rain received each day, week, or month. Compare their data to the totals given in the newspaper.

Video Project
What's with the Weather?

1. Watch the local weather report on a television station. What information is given
about today's weather?

_____

_____

_____

What information is given about tomorrow's weather?

_____

_____

_____

2. The local newspaper also gives information about the weather. Look up the weather
report to see what it says about today's and tomorrow's weather.

_____

_____

_____

_____

3. List four important facts given in both the newspaper and television weather reports.
Include these in your weather report.

1. _____

2. _____

3. _____

4. _____

4. Write a weather report.

_____

_____

_____

_____

_____

_____

_____

_____

_____

_____

5. List any props (numbers, symbols, pictures, or maps) you will use on your weather report.

_____

_____

_____

_____

_____

_____

_____

6. Practice your weather forecast several times before videotaping it.

7. Videotape your weather report.

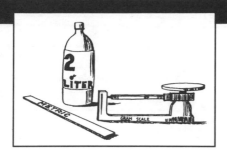

Math

Project Plan
Making It Metric

Objective
Students will produce a video explaining the metric system.

Equipment
- Video camera
- Tripod
- Microphone
- Audio mixer
- Sound source (tape deck, CD player, phonograph)
- Measuring devices
  1. Metric and English scales
  2. yardstick and meter stick

Procedure
Instructions for audio dubbing appear on pages 17–20.

1. Bring an empty half-gallon milk container and an empty 2-litre soda container to class. Ask students to identify the containers by their volume. Have them identify other common containers that hold English or metric amounts. (Water also comes in both English and metric containers.)

2. Distribute the Video Project: Making It Metric form. Encourage students to start collecting metric containers. (Tell them to wash the containers before bringing them to class!)

3. Give students ample time to weigh and measure themselves using both the metric and English scales and measures.

4. Students may work singly or in groups to make this video project. Or, make one class video, using different students for each section of the video (weighing and measuring, for example).

   Some of the shots of the scales and measurements should be done as macros so that adequate detail can be seen.

5. Encourage students to watch the recorded videotaped footage several times to be sure the script fits the video. Make script changes as needed.

6. Audio dub the script on the prerecorded footage.

Extension Activities
1. Encourage students to research other weights and measures used in the metric system (temperature, for example).

2. Allow students to research and compile a list of major industrial nations that use the metric system and compare that with a list of countries that use the English system of weights and measures.

3. Sponsor a metric olympics in your classroom.

Video Project
Making It Metric

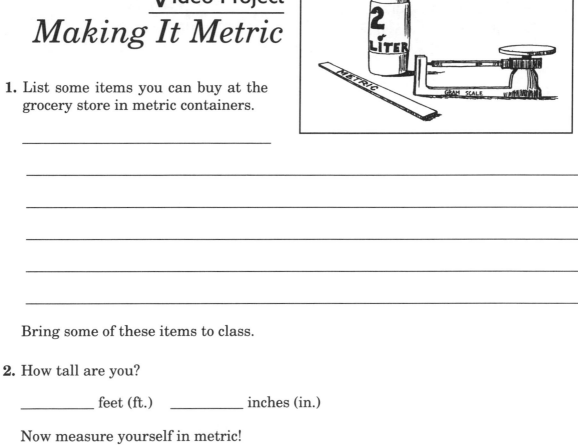

1. List some items you can buy at the grocery store in metric containers.

   _____

   _____

   _____

   _____

   _____

   _____

   Bring some of these items to class.

2. How tall are you?

   _____ feet (ft.)   _____ inches (in.)

   Now measure yourself in metric!

   _____ meters (m)   _____ centimeters (cm)

3. How much do you weigh?

   _____ pounds (lbs.)

   Now find a metric scale. How much do you weigh?

   _____ kilograms (kg)

4. What is the speed limit on the road in front of your school?

   _____ miles per hour (mph)

   What is this speed in kilometers per hour?

   _____ kilometers per hour (Km/h)

5. Write a script using the information you just learned about the metric system's weights and measures. Be sure to include:

- things we can buy in metric containers
- things we can measure in metric
- things we can weigh in metric
- how fast things can go in metric

6. List the camera shots you will need to go with your script.

1. _____

2. _____

3. _____

4. _____

5. _____

6. _____

7. _____

Add more shots if needed!

7. Videotape your camera shots.

8. Watch the recorded videotaped footage several times to be sure the script fits the video. Make scripts changes as needed.

9. Audio dub your script.

Math

Project Plan

It's the Same Amount—Volume!

Objective

The students will produce a video project illustrating the concept of volume as it relates to containers of various shapes.

Equipment

- Video camera
- Tripod
- Microphone
- Audio mixer
- Music source (tape deck, CD player, phonograph)

Procedure

1. Fill two glasses (one tall, thin glass and one short, fat glass) with equal amounts of water. Ask the students to identify which glass holds more, or are they the same?

2. Divide the class into groups of 3–5 students, or do this as a class activity. Distribute the Video Project: It's the Same Amount—Volume! form. Make sure each group has the necessary materials:
   - 3 glasses of various shapes
   - One 8-ounce measuring cup
   - Water

3. Allow students to begin the activity. They can complete steps 1 through 9 on the handout.

4. Discuss the results of their experiments.

5. Videotape the activity. Each group can do a video, or make one video as a class project.

6. Script: There are several ways of recording this activity:
   - Videotape the activity, and then audio dub the script.
   - Pin a lavaliere microphone (or use a shotgun mic) and have the students narrate as they perform the steps.
   - Have a student off camera narrate the tape as a student on camera performs the tasks.

Extension Activities

1. Perform the same experiment using jelly beans. Students can count the number of jelly beans in each glass. (Then they can eat them!)

2. Have the students take the experiment to a younger class, such as a kindergarten class. There they can amaze the younger crowd with their "magic."

Video Project

It's the Same Amount—Volume!

Many students believe that a tall glass holds more than a shorter glass. But taller does not mean bigger! Let's prove it by doing this video project.

1. This is what you will need to do this project:
   - Three 12-ounce glasses
        1 tall, thin glass
        1 medium glass
        1 short, fat glass
   - One 8-ounce measuring cup
   - Video camera

2. Place the three glasses next to each other in a row.

3. Fill the measuring cup with 8 ounces of water.

4. Pour the water into the shortest glass. See how full the glass is?

   How much water is in the glass? _____ ounces

5. Once again, fill the measuring cup with 8 ounces of water.

6. Pour the water into the medium glass. See how full the glass is?

   How much water is in the glass? _____ ounces

7. Once again fill the measuring cup with 8 ounces of water.

8. Pour the water into the tallest glass. See how full the glass is?

   How much water is in the glass? _____ ounces

9. Do all the glasses have the same amount of water in them?

_____ Yes   _____ No

How do you know? _____

Why do some of the glasses look more full?_____

10. Let's make a video of this experiment. Videotape each step as you do it.

What will be your first shot? _____

How will you end the video? _____

What will you say on the video? Write your script!

11. Videotape the experiment. Audio dub your script on the videotape.

Safety and Health

P roject Plan
Signs of Safety

Objective
Students will produce a video project about safety signs and their meanings.

Equipment
- Video camera
- Tripod
- Audio mixer
- Music source (tape deck, CD player, phonograph)
- Microphone

Procedure
Detailed instructions for making macro projects, including title cards, appear on pages 12–17. Instructions for audio dubbing appear on pages 17–20.

1. Take the students on a short walk around the school and point out some safety signs. These might include stop signs, school bus signs, or school crossing signs. Remind students to bring pencil and paper, and allow plenty of time for them to sketch each sign. Discuss what the signs mean, why there are no words on some of them, and how they help drivers.

2. Distribute the Video Project: Signs of Safety form. Encourage the students to draw as well as they can the safety signs they observed around the school or neighborhood. You might want to get a few instructional manuals from your local driver's license bureau so students can look up the meaning of some of the signs.

3. Record a title card.

4. Allow the students to videotape the signs. Instruct them to record enough footage of each sign so they'll have enough time for their script. About 12–15 seconds per sign should be adequate. *Or*, allow students to photograph the signs and then videotape the photographs.

5. Students should review their footage and practice their script before audio dubbing.

6. Have students audio dub their project.

Extension Activities
1. Have the students create construction paper copies of their signs, hold the signs up in front of the class, and have classmates guess the signs' meanings.

2. Invite a local police officer to class to explain traffic signs and to answer students' questions about signs and safety.

3. Have your class sponsor a Safety Signs Poster Contest in your school. How will signs be judged? What will be the prize?

From *Video Projects for Elementary and Middle Schools.* © 1995 Keith Kyker and Christopher Curchy. Libraries Unlimited. (800) 237-6124.

Video Project
Signs of Safety

1. Look at the drawing. Have you ever seen one of these signs?

   What does it mean? _____

   _____

   _____

2. Take a walk around your school or neighborhood and make a drawing of six safety signs you see. Make sure you take along paper and pencil!

Draw the signs here.	**What does each sign mean?**
Sign 1	_____
	_____
	_____
Sign 2	_____
	_____
	_____
Sign 3	_____
	_____
	_____

Sign 4   _____

                                             _____

                                             _____

Sign 5   _____

                                             _____

                                             _____

Sign 6   _____

                                             _____

                                             _____

3. Now you can make a video project about these signs of safety. Here are the steps in your project:

Step 1   Make a title card.

Step 2   Videotape each safety sign for at least 12–15 seconds.

Step 3   Write a script describing each sign and its meaning.

Step 4   Audio dub your script onto your tape. Your script will include the description of each sign and its meaning.

Safety and Health

Project Plan
Making a Healthy Lunch

Objective

Students will produce a video project demonstrating how to make a healthy lunch.

Equipment

- Video camera
- Tripod
- Audio mixer
- Music source (tape deck, CD player, phonograph)
- Microphone

Procedure

Instructions for audio dubbing appear on pages 17–20.

1. Ask students to tell about their favorite lunches. What kinds of food do they like in their lunches? What does *healthy* mean? What makes a lunch healthy?

2. Distribute the Video Project: Making a Healthy Lunch form. Read it over with your students and allow them time to answer the questions.

3. Discuss their answers. Allow a few students to read their scripts aloud. What kinds of foods did they list? What materials are needed to make lunches?

4. After the scripts have been written, allow students to videotape their project. Encourage using some different camera angles (over the shoulder, close-ups, or macro shots) to make the project interesting.

    Plan to answer these questions:

    - Who will bring in the items for videotaping? When?
    - Who will bring in packing materials, such as sandwich bags, plastic wrap, aluminum foil, and so forth?
    - Can students eat their lunches after they complete their project?

5. Have students practice reading their scripts aloud as they watch the videotaped footage.

6. Have students audio dub the scripts on the videotaped footage.

Extension Activities

1. Talk about food groups. Have students draw or paint a healthy lunch that includes at least one food from each food group.

2. Invite a nutritionist (volunteer, school nurse, or knowledgeable parent) to talk about the fat content of foods. Show students how to read the nutritional labels on some of their favorite foods. Let students compare the fat content of some of their favorite foods. How much of a difference is there between low-fat foods and regular foods?

3. Survey another class to find out their favorite foods. Which are healthy foods and which are not?

4. Ask your local McDonald's or Burger King to supply you with the nutritional information of some of their foods. Have students compare these lunches to their healthy lunches.

Video Project
Making a Healthy Lunch

1. What are some of the foods you would put in a healthy lunch?

_____

_____

_____

_____

_____

2. What are some things that do *not* belong in a healthy lunch?

_____

_____

_____

_____

3. How would you wrap or pack each food to keep it fresh?

_____

_____

_____

4. Would you need to keep anything cold so it would not spoil? How can you do that?

_____

_____

_____

5. Write a story telling someone how to make a healthy lunch. This will be the script for your project.

6. List all the items you need to make your healthy lunch.

_____

_____

_____

_____

_____

7. Write down six camera shots you need for your video project.

1. _____

2. _____

3. _____

4. _____

5. _____

6. _____

8. Videotape your project.

9. Practice your script as you watch your videotape.

10. Audio dub your script on your videotape.

Safety and Health

Project Plan
Safety on the Field

Objective
Students will produce a video project demonstrating four safety tips for playing a particular sport.

Equipment
- Video camera
- Tripod
- Audio mixer
- Sound source (tape deck, CD player, phonograph)
- Microphone

Procedure
Instructions for audio dubbing appear on pages 17–20.

1. Bring in some sports equipment that is used to protect players from injury, for example:

    - Baseball/softball—helmet, catcher's mask, shin guards
    - Hockey—pads, helmet, goalie mask
    - Gymnastics—grips, ankle brace
    - Skating—knee pads, gloves

    Discuss how safety equipment is used to guard against injuries. Have the students identify tips that help protect athletes from injuries.

2. Distribute the Video Project: Safety on the Field form. Read it over with students and allow them to complete the form.

3. Suggest each student or group make a list of any equipment needed to complete their videotaping. Perhaps the physical education teacher or classmates can assist in finding the necessary equipment.

4. Because most of the videotaping will be outside or on the field, you may want to enlist the assistance of the coach or a parent to supervise the videotaping.

5. Make sure the students are shooting enough tape to audio dub their tips. Each shot should be 5–10 seconds longer than their tip when it is read aloud.

6. Have students bring in their equipment before the scheduled date of videotaping. This way they can make sure everything works or fits.

7. After students have videotaped their shots, have them rehearse their script several times before audio dubbing their script.

8. Have students audio dub their video project.

Extension Activities

1. Many instructional sports videos include safety tips. Ask local video rental stores to provide some instructional videos about golf, gymnastics, tennis, or other sports for your students to watch. What safety tips did the videos include?

2. Invite a local pediatrician to speak to the class about the number or type of injuries children suffer because they do not use the proper equipment when playing sports.

3. Have the students sponsor a schoolwide safety poster contest. Ask a local sporting goods store to donate some safety equipment for prizes. Enlist the support of your school PTA to donate prizes.

From *Video Projects for Elementary and Middle Schools.* © 1995 Keith Kyker and Christopher Curchy. Libraries Unlimited. (800) 237-6124.

Video Project
Safety on the Field

1. What sport(s) do you like to play?

_____

_____

2. Write four safety tips you need to remember when playing this sport.
    Example: Tennis
        Safety tip 1: Wear a good pair of sneakers or tennis shoes.
        Safety tip 2: Have plenty of water or fluids on hand for drinking.

Safety tip 1 _____

_____

Safety tip 2 _____

_____

Safety tip 3 _____

_____

Safety tip 4 _____

_____

3. Write a script for your video project. Be sure to start with a good opening sentence. Then include your four safety tips. Finish with a concluding sentence.

4. Make a list of the camera shots you will need.

What will be your opening shot? _____

_____

_____

_____

What shots do you need for your safety tips?

Tip 1 _____

Tip 2 _____

Tip 3 _____

Tip 4 _____

What will be your ending shot? _____

_____

_____

5. Videotape your shots.

6. Rehearse your script while you watch your videotape. Then audio dub your script onto your footage.

P̲roject Plan

Learning to Play _____ !

Objective

Students will produce a video project that informs others about a sport, its equipment, and some of its rules.

Equipment

- Video camera
- Tripod
- Audio mixer
- Music source (tape deck, CD player, phonograph)
- Microphone
- Sporting equipment

Procedure

Detailed instructions for making macro projects, including title cards, appear on pages 12–17. Instructions for audio dubbing appear on pages 17–20.

1. Ask students what their favorite sport is? Make a list on the board or an overhead.

2. Distribute the Video Project: Learning to Play _____ ! form. Let students read over the form. Students who enjoy similar sports may work together on the project.

3. Give students ample time to complete the video project form. Some students may want to go to the media center to locate a book about their sport.

4. This video project will probably be videotaped outside, most likely on a field or playground. Allow students to check with the coach about scheduling a date for videotaping.

5. What equipment does each group need? Is this readily available at the school, or will the students need to bring equipment from home? Where will it be stored?

6. It is important that the students work from a well-written script. Have them practice their script and use it as a guide to assist them in identifying what shots are needed. Have them time the script so they can get an idea of how long each shot should be taped. Shots that are too long will be boring, while shots that are too short will not fit the script.

7. Schedule your students' taping days. Ask a parent or school volunteer to help students with videotaping. Students may ask classmates to serve as extras on the field or in the stands.

8. Once the footage has been taped, allow the students to practice their script while watching their video. Some script changes might need to be made at this time.

9. Audio dub the script onto the videotape.

10. Watch the videos.

Extension Activities

1. Bring in an instructional video of a sport. You can rent these at most local video stores. Allow the students to view this tape. What are some things that are similar to their projects? What was done differently?

2. Have your students read a biography about a famous sports athlete. Let them tell the class about this athlete and what they learned about his or her life.

3. Invite the physical education teacher to watch the videos!

Video Project
Learning to Play _____ !

1. What is your favorite sport?

   _____

2. List the equipment you need to play this sport.

   _____

   _____

   _____

3. What are some important skills you need to play this sport? For example, in softball you need to be able to bat, throw, and catch a ball.

   _____

   _____

   _____

   _____

   _____

4. List three rules you need to follow when you play this sport. For example, in golf, the player suffers a penalty for moving the ball.

   Rule 1 _____

   _____

   Rule 2 _____

   _____

   Rule 3 _____

   _____

5. How will your video begin? What will your first camera shot be?

_____

6. Write a script for your video. Pretend you are actually telling a friend how to play this sport. Be sure to include:
  - the name of the sport
  - the equipment you need to play the sport
  - some of the rules you must follow to play this sport

7. Make a list of the camera shots you will need for your video. How long will each shot be?

8. Make a title card for your project. Then videotape your camera shots.

9. Practice your script as you watch your videotape. Then audio dub your script on your tape.

Physical Education

Project Plan

Exercise—What's Good for You?

Objective

The students will produce a video project demonstrating the benefits of exercise.

Equipment

- Video camera
- Tripod
- Audio mixer
- Sound source (tape deck, CD player, phonograph)
- Microphone

Procedure

Instructions for audio dubbing appear on pages 17–20.

1. Ask the students whether or not they exercise. Do their parents? What kinds of exercise can they identify?

2. Distribute the Video Project: Exercise—What's Good for You? form. Have students complete items 1–3. Discuss their answers.

3. Allow students ample time to write their script and plan their video. Some considerations should include:
   - Schedule students for taping dates and times. Be sure all the students have the materials and equipment they need.
   - Practice might be a good idea, especially if the students aren't familiar with a specific form of exercise. For example, aerobics look easy until you try them.
   - Some of these projects might be recorded live; that is, the students may give directions as they do the exercises, such as calisthenics or aerobics. Select and use microphones accordingly.

4. After students have recorded the video footage, have them rehearse their script while watching the video.

5. Audio dub the script onto the recorded footage.

Extension Activities

1. Obtain some exercise videos from your local video store. Watch them and have students discuss the following aspects:

   - What skills are taught?
   - How are the commercial videos similar to the students' exercise videos? How are they different?
   - Would the students buy these videos? Why?

2. Invite the physical education teacher or a local YMCA exercise coordinator to speak to the class about exercise. Ask the visitor to teach students some forms of exercise.

3. Have students design an exercise schedule for themselves. Have them keep track of the days, times, and types of exercises they complete. Was it hard to stay on schedule? (For fun, let them design a schedule for you. Good luck!)

Video Project

Exercise—What's Good for You?

1. Why should people exercise? List three reasons.

    1. _____

    2. _____

    3. _____

2. What are some of the ways people exercise?

_____

_____

_____

_____

_____

3. What can happen to people who do not exercise?

_____

_____

Planning Your Video

4. Write your script. How will your video begin? What exercise(s) will you demonstrate? How will your video end?

5. Make a list of the video shots you will need. Be sure each shot is long enough for your script.

6. What will the actors need to wear in the video? Make a list.

7. Do you need any exercise equipment for your video? Add this to your list.

8. Videotape your footage.

9. Watch your videotaped footage. Practice reading your script. Audio dub your script on your videotape.

Art

Project Plan
Artist of the Week

Objective

The students will produce a video project highlighting a student artist and her or his artwork.

Equipment

- Video camera
- Tripod
- Audio mixer
- Sound source (tape deck, CD player, phonograph)
- Microphone

Procedure

Detailed instructions for making macro projects, including title cards, appear on pages 12–17. Instructions for audio dubbing appear on pages 17–20.

1. From the art teacher obtain several examples of artwork by students. Try to get artwork in a variety of media (pen, crayon, paint, watercolor, clay). Show the artwork to your students. Discuss what is good about the artwork, the students who made the artwork, and some good artwork that your students have seen.

2. Distribute the Video Project: Artist of the Week form. Allow students time to complete items 1 and 2. Discuss the answers with the students.

3. Enlist the assistance of the art teacher for this project. Consider making Artist of the Week a regular feature on your news show.

4. Assist the students in scheduling times to videotape their artists. Consider scheduling the videotaping during the artist's regularly scheduled art class.
   - Tripods should be used to record the artwork.
   - Paintings and drawings videotape well using the macro lens.

5. Encourage students to practice reading their scripts as they watch the recorded footage.

6. Have students audio dub the script and music on their videotapes.

Extension Activities

1. Invite a local artist to demonstrate creating a project in your classroom. Perhaps a student who works in the same media as the artist could help demonstrate.

2. Have students research the lives of some famous artists, write a short biographical essay about the artist, and show some of the artist's work. Many libraries circulate prints of famous paintings.

3. Sidewalk art can be fun to make and look at. Chalk made for this activity can be purchased at local retail stores. Ask the Artist of the Week to do a sidewalk drawing for everyone to see. (Get permission first.) This can also be videotaped!

Video Project
Artist of the Week

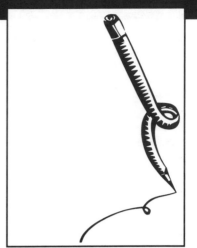

1. Are there any artists in your class? In your grade? In your school? How can you find out?

    _____

    _____

    _____

2. What would you like to know about this artist? Try to find out at least three things about the artist and his or her artwork. Ask the artist, the art teacher, the artist's classroom teacher, or the artist's parents.

    1. _____

    2. _____

    3. _____

Planning Your Project

3. Videotape the artist at work. This can be done in the classroom or in the art room. Record about 20–30 seconds. Try to get two or three camera angles.

4. Videotape several pieces of the artist's work. Select 4 or 5 pieces and record each one for 6–10 seconds.

5. Audio dub the information about the artist over the footage of him or her working. Then audio dub music only over the shots of the artist's work.

6. Review the finished project.

Art

Project Plan
Hey! It's Clay!

Objective

The students will produce a video project that illustrates how clay is used to make various art projects.

Equipment

- Video camera
- Tripod
- Audio mixer
- Sound source (tape deck, CD player, phonograph)
- Microphone

Procedure

Instructions for audio dubbing appear on pages 17–20.

1. Pass around some small pieces of clay. Ask the students to describe the clay and how it is used to make works of art. (Most students have had clay experiences in art classes at school. If not, perhaps you can request the art teacher to assist your class in making clay pieces of art.) Talk about the process of getting from a clay ball to a clay figure. Ask the art teacher to make a few sample pieces for you to show the students.

2. Distribute the Video Project: Hey! It's Clay! form. Give students ample time to complete the form. They might have to research the use of a kiln if they are not familiar with it. They can ask the art teacher about the use of a kiln in making clay art objects.

3. Ask the art teacher to assist in this project. Schedule your videotaping sessions with the art teacher. Or, complete this project in your classroom. Clay can be purchased inexpensively in bulk at art supply retailers.

4. After students have videotaped their footage, have them rehearse their script while previewing their footage.

5. Help students audio dub the narration and music on their videotaped footage.

Extension Activities

1. Invite a local potter to demonstrate some techniques and show samples of finished pieces to your class. Students are always intrigued watching someone throw a pot on a wheel. Videotape this guest's demonstration for your school's art teacher.

2. How did Native Americans, nomadic tribesmen, and others make clay pots without the use of kilns? These techniques make an interesting topic for research.

3. Visit a local art gallery to see professional artists' work on display.

Video Project
Hey! It's Clay!

1. Have you ever made figures, shapes, or pots and bowls out of clay? What are some of the steps you went through to make these things?

_____

_____

_____

_____

_____

2. What is a kiln?

_____

Does your school have one? _____

3. Let's plan a video project showing how students can use clay to make fun and interesting projects!

Step 1   Write a three-to-five-sentence introduction that describes some of the steps you must do to make projects out of clay. This will be your script.

Step 2   Videotape a student doing the steps in your script. Be sure to videotape each shot you will need.

Step 3   Videotape several (5–10) completed projects students have made out of clay.

Step 4   Audio dub your script on the part of the video project showing the steps to make a clay project. Audio dub music *only* over the section of the videotape showing the completed projects.

P roject Plan
What Our Principal Does

Objective

The students will videotape an interview with the school principal.

Equipment

- Video camera
- Tripod
- Microphone
- Headphones (to check microphone sound)

Procedure

1. Discuss the role of the school principal with your students. Ask them to help you create a list of some of the jobs a school principal does. Write down their suggestions on the chalkboard or on an overhead.

2. Distribute the Video Project: What Our Principal Does form. Allow students time to complete the form. Some of the following suggestions might assist your students in this project:

    - Discuss the concept of open-ended questions (see the example on page 111). Help students write their questions.

    - Let students practice their interviews in the classroom. One student (or you) can role-play the principal. This is good practice for the videographer, too. Record a few practice interviews and let students critique their styles in terms of:

        1. microphone placement
        2. eye contact with guest or camera
        3. familiarity with their questions
        4. diction and speed of delivery

3. This project can be adapted to any school worker. Students can work in teams of two (reporter and videographer) to conduct interviews with all of your school workers.

Extension Activities

1. Record an interview or two from a local news station. Critique the reporters' styles in terms of:

    - introduction
    - questions asked
    - closing
    - eye contact with guest or camera

2. Invite a local radio or television news reporter to speak to students about interviewing guests on camera. Ask the guest to bring a videotape of some of their interviews.

3. Have students prepare for an interview with a famous person in American history. Have them answer the following questions:
   - Who are you interviewing? (You may assign persons students have studied or will study during the school year.)
   - How will you introduce your subject?
   - What questions will you ask?
   - How will you close?

Video Project

What Our Principal Does

1. What is your principal's name?

_____

2. What are some of the jobs your principal does at your school? Can you think of at least three?

_____

_____

_____

3. Interview the principal. Here are some of the things you will have to think about before you interview the principal:

- Write down four questions you would like to ask your principal. Make sure your questions are interesting and cannot be answered with only one or two words.

    Good: What are some things you like about being a principal?

    Bad: Do you like being a principal?

    Question 1 _____

    _____

    _____

    Question 2 _____

    _____

    _____

    Question 3 _____

    _____

    _____

Question 4 _____

_____

_____

- How will you introduce yourself and the principal? Here is a sample introduction:

    "Good morning. I'm Stacy Johnson and with me is principal William Roberts. Today we will be talking with Mr. Roberts about his job as principal of Oak Hill Elementary School."

Write your introduction:

_____

_____

_____

_____

- A good interview also needs a closing. If you are doing an interview for a school news show, you should mention the name of your show in your closing.

    Here is an example of a closing:

    "Thank you Mr. Johnson, for telling us more about your job as principal of Oak Hill Elementary School. It certainly sounds like it is both fun and challenging. Reporting for Eagle Channel News, I'm Stacy Roberts."

Write a closing for your interview:

_____

_____

_____

_____

- Write a short letter to your principal requesting a time/date when you can come to their office for your interview.

- Be sure to thank the principal when you have completed your interview!

This project can be done with any school worker: secretary, bookkeeper, lunchroom manager, janitor, bus driver.

Project Plan
Teacher of the Week

Objective
The students will videotape an interview with a teacher selected as "Teacher of the Week."

Equipment
- Video camera
- Tripod
- Microphone
- Headphones (to check microphone sound)

Procedure
1. Ask the students about some of their favorite teachers. What did those teachers do to make learning fun and interesting?
2. Distribute the Video Project: Teacher of the Week form. Allow students time to complete the form. Some of the following suggestions might assist your students with this project:
   - Discuss the concept of open-ended questions (see the example on page 114). Help students write open-ended questions.
   - Let students practice their interviews in the classroom. One student (or you) can role-play the teacher. This is good practice for the videographer, too! Record a few practice interviews and let students critique their interviewing techniques in terms of:
     1. microphone placement
     2. eye contact with guest or camera
     3. familiarity with their questions
     4. diction and speed of delivery
3. A good adaption of this project would be Student of the Week.

Extension Activities
1. Have students take a photograph of the Teacher of the Week and create a bulletin board somewhere on campus. Have them take a few photographs of the teacher working with students.
2. Invite a local news reporter to give your students some suggestions and tips for interviewing and for videotaping interviews.

Video Project
Teacher of the Week

1. Do you have a favorite teacher?

Who is it? _____

2. What are some of the things this teacher does in the classroom that make learning fun and interesting?

_____

_____

_____

_____

_____

_____

3. Interview this teacher. Here are some of the things you will have to think about before you interview the teacher.

- What questions will you ask this teacher? Write down four questions you would like to ask during this interview. Make sure your questions are interesting and cannot be answered with only one or two words.

  Good: Why do you like to teach math?

  Bad: Do you like teaching math?

  Question 1 _____

  _____

  Question 2 _____

  _____

Question 3 _____

_____

Question 4 _____

_____

- How will you introduce this teacher? Here is a sample introduction:

  "Good morning! Our Teacher of the Week is Ms. Quinn. Ms. Quinn teaches eighth-grade English and really enjoys reading."

Write your introduction:

_____

_____

_____

_____

_____

- A good interview needs a closing. If you are doing an interview for a school news show, you should include the name of your show in the closing.

  Here is an example of a closing:

  "Thank you, Ms. Quinn, for telling us more about yourself and your teaching. Congratulations on being chosen as our Teacher of the Week. Reporting for Eagle Channel News, I'm Brad Crosby."

Write a closing for your interview:

_____

_____

_____

_____

- Schedule a day and time to interview the Teacher of the Week. Be sure to thank your guest after the interview.

Project Plan
How We Get to School

Objective
Students will produce a video describing how students arrive at school each day.

Equipment
- Video camera
- Tripod
- Audio mixer
- Sound source (tape deck, CD player, phonograph)
- Microphone

Procedure
Detailed instructions for making macro projects, including title cards, appear on pages 12–17. Instructions for audio dubbing appear on pages 17–20.

1. Discuss with students the various ways students arrive at school each morning (walk, ride a bus, carpool, or other).
2. Distribute the Video Project: How We Get to School form. Give the students ample time to complete the form.
3. Help students write and proofread their scripts.
4. Schedule videotaping. Some suggestions include:
   - Students may need to make arrangements to get to school early on their taping date.
   - Be sure to schedule this video project during early fall or late spring, when it is light enough in the early morning hours for videotaping.
   - Students should get one or two shots of each mode of transportation students use to get to school. Don't forget students who walk to school.
   - This project can easily be adapted to a macro project. Students can take photographs and videotape the pictures.
5. After students have completed videotaping, encourage them to rehearse their script while watching the videotape.
6. Have students audio dub the script onto the videotape.

Extension Activities
1. Invite a bus driver to talk to the class about driving a school bus as a career. Are there students in the class who have never ridden a school bus? When was the first school bus used in the United States? How have school buses changed in the last 20 years?

2. Many schools use safety patrols and crossing guards to help students as they arrive and depart the campus. Have your students interview these student or adult volunteers about their role in school safety.

3. Survey several classes to find out the percentage of students that use the following ways of arriving to school each day:

   - walk
   - ride the bus
   - come to school in a car
   - ride a bicycle
   - some combination

Video Project
How We Get to School

1. How do you get to school each day?

_____

_____

2. What are some other ways students arrive at your school each day?

_____

_____

_____

_____

_____

3. Write a story about how students arrive at school each day. Be sure to include all the ways students use to get to school. This will be your script for your video project.

4. Make a list of the camera shots you will need for your project. Compare this list to your script to be sure you have each shot you will need for your script.

5. Videotape the camera shots you have on your list. Be sure each one is videotaped long enough to fit your script.

6. Rehearse your script as you watch your videotape. Audio dub your script onto your videotape.

Index